JavaScript Handbook

Advanced Functions

Unlocking JavaScript: Advanced Functionality

By

Laurence Lars Svekis

Dedicated to

Alexis and Sebastian

Thank you for your support

For more content and to learn more, visit

https://basescripts.com/

JavaScript Handbook
Advanced Functions

Summary

"JavaScript Handbook: Advanced Functions" delves into the essential concepts and practices that elevate JavaScript from a basic scripting language to a tool for building sophisticated, maintainable, and scalable applications.

Covering topics like higher-order functions, currying, composition, and functional programming principles, this book is designed to help developers write cleaner and more reusable code. Through clear explanations, hands-on examples, and exercises, it bridges the gap between theory and practical application. Whether you're optimizing existing projects or crafting new solutions, this guide empowers you with the knowledge to succeed in modern JavaScript development.

Introduction

Welcome to "JavaScript Handbook: Advanced Functions", a comprehensive exploration of some of the most powerful and versatile tools in JavaScript. This book is tailored for developers who want to deepen their understanding of advanced JavaScript concepts, including higher-order functions, currying, composition, and more.

From real-world examples to coding exercises, you'll learn how these advanced techniques can make your code more modular, readable, and maintainable. Whether you're a seasoned developer or an ambitious learner, this book will expand your JavaScript toolkit, enabling you to write cleaner, more efficient, and reusable code.

Understanding Higher-Order Functions in JavaScript

What Are Higher-Order Functions?

In JavaScript, **higher-order functions** are functions that either:
1. **Take one or more functions as arguments**, or
2. **Return a new function as a result** (or both).

This concept is at the heart of functional programming and greatly contributes to code reusability, modularity, and expressive power.

Common Examples of Higher-Order Functions

- **Array methods like `map()`, `filter()`, `reduce()`**: These methods accept functions as arguments.
- **Event handlers and callbacks**: Passing a function to `addEventListener()` in the browser or `setTimeout()` in Node.js is using a higher-order function.
- **Function decorators and wrappers**: A function that takes another function and returns a modified version of it.

Why Use Higher-Order Functions?

- **Abstraction**: They allow you to abstract operations on data sets.
- **Reusability**: Write general-purpose functions that can be customized by passing in different functions.
- **Cleaner Code**: Reduce boilerplate and make code more declarative.

Examples of Higher-Order Functions

Passing a function as an argument:

```
function greet(name) {
    console.log("Hello, " + name);
}
function sayHello(func, person) {
    func(person); // func is a function passed as
an argument
```

```
}
sayHello(greet, "Alice"); // "Hello, Alice"
```
Returning a function:

```
function multiplier(factor) {
  return function(x) {
    return x * factor;
  };
}
const double = multiplier(2);
console.log(double(5)); // 10
```
Array methods:

```
let numbers = [1, 2, 3, 4];
let doubled = numbers.map((num) => num * 2); //
map takes a function as an argument
console.log(doubled); // [2, 4, 6, 8]
let evenNumbers = numbers.filter((num) => num % 2
=== 0);
console.log(evenNumbers); // [2, 4]
```
Callbacks:

```
setTimeout(() => {
  console.log("This runs after 1 second");
}, 1000);
```

Function that returns a decorator:

```javascript
function once(fn) {
  let done = false;
  return function(...args) {
    if (!done) {
      done = true;
      return fn(...args);
    }
  };
}
let logOnce = once((msg) => console.log(msg));
logOnce("First call"); // "First call"
logOnce("Second call"); // no output because fn
only runs once
```

Tips for Using Higher-Order Functions

- Keep your callback functions pure and simple.
- Use arrow functions for concise inline definitions.
- Think in terms of data transformations rather than loops—
map, filter, reduce are powerful abstractions.

Multiple-Choice Questions

1.   **What is a Higher-Order Function in JavaScript?**
A. A function that only takes numbers as arguments.

B. A function that returns a promise.

C. A function that takes or returns another function.

D. A function that only runs once.

Answer: C

Explanation: Higher-order functions are defined by their ability to take functions as arguments or return them.

2.   **Which of the following array methods is a higher-order function?**

A. `push()`

B. `pop()`

C. `map()`

D. `length` property

Answer: C

Explanation: `map()` takes a function as an argument, making it higher-order.

3.   **In `array.map(fn)`, what is fn?**

A. A callback function provided to map.

B. A string.

C. The array length.

D. A boolean value.

Answer: A

Explanation: `map()` expects a callback function that it applies to each element.

What does the following function return?

```
function add(a) {
    return function(b) {
```

```
    return a + b;
  };
}
```

4.   A. A number

B. An object

C. A function

D. Undefined

Answer: C

Explanation: add(a) returns a function that takes b and returns a+b.

5.   **Which statement best describes filter()?**

A. It changes the original array.

B. It returns a new array with elements that satisfy the given condition.

C. It always returns a single value.

D. It only works on strings.

Answer: B

Explanation: filter() returns a new array of elements for which the callback returns true.

6.   **reduce() in JavaScript:** A. Takes a callback and reduces the array to a single value.

B. Always returns an array.

C. Does not allow initial values.

D. Returns the largest element of the array.

Answer: A

Explanation: reduce() applies a function against an accumulator to reduce the array to a single value.

B. A function that returns a promise.

C. A function that takes or returns another function.

D. A function that only runs once.

Answer: C

Explanation: Higher-order functions are defined by their ability to take functions as arguments or return them.

2.   **Which of the following array methods is a higher-order function?**

A. push()

B. pop()

C. map()

D. length property

Answer: C

Explanation: map() takes a function as an argument, making it higher-order.

3.   **In array.map(fn), what is fn?**

A. A callback function provided to map.

B. A string.

C. The array length.

D. A boolean value.

Answer: A

Explanation: map() expects a callback function that it applies to each element.

What does the following function return?

```
function add(a) {
   return function(b) {
```

```
        return a + b;
    };
}
```

4.   A. A number

B. An object

C. A function

D. Undefined

Answer: C

Explanation: `add(a)` returns a function that takes b and returns a+b.

5.   **Which statement best describes `filter()`?**

A. It changes the original array.

B. It returns a new array with elements that satisfy the given condition.

C. It always returns a single value.

D. It only works on strings.

Answer: B

Explanation: `filter()` returns a new array of elements for which the callback returns true.

6.   **`reduce()` in JavaScript:** A. Takes a callback and reduces the array to a single value.

B. Always returns an array.

C. Does not allow initial values.

D. Returns the largest element of the array.

Answer: A

Explanation: `reduce()` applies a function against an accumulator to reduce the array to a single value.

7. **Which of the following is NOT a higher-order function usage?**

A. Passing a function as an argument.

B. Returning a function from another function.

C. Storing a function in a variable.

D. Writing a function that takes no arguments.

Answer: D

Explanation: A function that takes no arguments isn't necessarily higher-order. Higher-order relates to functions as arguments or return values.

8. **What does setTimeout() exemplify in JavaScript?**

A. A pure function

B. A higher-order function that takes a callback

C. A synchronous iteration method

D. A function that returns another function

Answer: B

Explanation: setTimeout() takes a function (callback) as an argument, making it higher-order.

9. **What is a callback function?**

A. A function that is passed as an argument to another function.

B. A function that runs immediately upon definition.

C. A function that never returns a value.

D. A function that only works with promises.

Answer: A

Explanation: A callback is a function passed into another function to be invoked later.

10. **once(fn) is a higher-order function that:** A. Runs the given function multiple times.

B. Returns a new function that runs `fn` only once.

C. Immediately calls `fn`.

D. Does not accept functions as arguments.

Answer: B

Explanation: `once(fn)` returns a function that ensures `fn` runs at most once.

11. **If `functionA` returns `functionB`, what can we say about `functionA`?**

A. It is a callback.

B. It is a higher-order function.

C. It is a promise.

D. It is a pure function only.

Answer: B

Explanation: Returning a function makes `functionA` a higher-order function.

12. **Which built-in JavaScript functions are considered higher-order?**

A. `alert()`

B. `parseInt()`

C. `Array.prototype.map()`

D. `Math.max()`

Answer: C

Explanation: `map()` accepts a function as an argument, thus is higher-order.

13. **What does the `reduce()` callback function receive as arguments?**

A. The current element only

B. The accumulator, current element, current index, and the entire array

C. Only the initial accumulator value

D. No arguments

Answer: B

Explanation: The reduce() callback gets (accumulator, currentValue, currentIndex, array).

14.   **Higher-order functions are closely related to which programming paradigm?**

A. Object-Oriented Programming

B. Functional Programming

C. Procedural Programming

D. Assembly-level programming

Answer: B

Explanation: Higher-order functions are a key concept in functional programming.

15.   **What is the return value of ["a","b","c"].map((x) => x.toUpperCase())?**

A. A transformed array ["A","B","C"]

B. The original array ["a","b","c"]

C. A single string

D. Undefined

Answer: A

Explanation: map() returns a new array with the transformation applied.

16.   **Can a higher-order function be anonymous?**

A. No, it must be named.

B. Yes, it can use arrow functions or unnamed function expressions.

C. Only if defined at the global scope.

D. It must always be assigned to a variable.

Answer: B

Explanation: Higher-order functions can be anonymous, e.g., using arrow functions.

17.   **Which method stops execution after finding a matching element?** A. `map()`

B. `forEach()`

C. `find()`

D. `filter()`

Answer: C

Explanation: `find()` returns the first found element and then stops.

What does the following code log?

```
[1,2,3].filter(x => x > 1).map(x => x * 2)
```

18.   A. `[2, 4, 6]`

B. `[4, 6]`

C. `[1, 2, 3]`

D. `[4]`

Answer: A

Explanation: `filter(x > 1)` gives `[2,3]`, `map(x*2)` on that gives `[4,6]`. Wait, carefully re-check. The original array is `[1,2,3]`. Filter x > 1 returns `[2, 3]`. Then map x * 2 on `[2,`

3] gives [4, 6]. The correct answer is [4, 6], not [2,4,6].

Correction: The correct answer is **[4, 6]**.

19.   **If you have a function decorate(fn) that returns a new function wrapping fn, what is decorate?**

A. A normal function

B. A higher-order function (it returns a function)

C. A promise

D. A class

Answer: B

Explanation: Returning a new function makes decorate a higher-order function.

20.   **forEach() vs map():** A. Both return new arrays.

B. forEach() returns undefined, map() returns a new array.

C. forEach() and map() return the same result.

D. forEach() returns the original array, map() returns a new array.

Answer: B

Explanation: forEach() returns undefined, while map() returns a new array.

10 Coding Exercises with Full Solutions and Explanations

Exercise 1: Create a Higher-Order Function that Returns a Function

Task: Write a function `multiplyBy(factor)` that returns a new function that multiplies its argument by `factor`.

Solution:

```
function multiplyBy(factor) {
    return function(num) {
        return num * factor;
    };
}
const triple = multiplyBy(3);
console.log(triple(10)); // 30
```

Explanation: `multiplyBy` is a HOF because it returns a function.

Exercise 2: Using Array.map with a Callback

Task: Given an array of numbers `[1,2,3]`, use `map()` to create an array of their squares.

Solution:

```
let arr = [1,2,3];
let squares = arr.map(x => x*x);
console.log(squares); // [1,4,9]
```

Explanation: `map()` takes a callback function, making it a higher-order function.

Exercise 3: Implement a `filterEven` Function Using `filter()`

Task: Write a function `filterEven(numbers)` that uses `filter()` to return only even numbers.

Solution:

```
function filterEven(numbers) {
    return numbers.filter(num => num % 2 === 0);
}
console.log(filterEven([1,2,3,4,5,6])); //
[2,4,6]
```

Explanation: `filter()` is a HOF that takes a function to determine which elements to keep.

Exercise 4: Create a once Higher-Order Function

Task: `once(fn)` should return a new function that calls `fn` only the first time and ignores subsequent calls.

Solution:

```
function once(fn) {
    let called = false;
    return function(...args) {
        if (!called) {
            called = true;
            return fn(...args);
        }
    };
}
let onlyOnce = once((msg) => console.log(msg));
onlyOnce("Hello"); // "Hello"
onlyOnce("World"); // no output
```

Explanation: once returns a new function, making it a HOF.

Exercise 5: Use `reduce()` to Sum an Array

Task: Use `reduce()` to sum the numbers in $[1,2,3,4]$.

Solution:

```
let sum = [1,2,3,4].reduce((acc, val) => acc +
val, 0);
console.log(sum); // 10
```

Explanation: `reduce()` is a HOF, taking a callback that processes each element.

Exercise 6: Create a Function that Takes a Callback

Task: Create a function `applyTwice(fn, value)` that applies fn to value twice.

Solution:

```
function applyTwice(fn, value) {
   return fn(fn(value));
}
function add2(x) {
   return x + 2;
}
console.log(applyTwice(add2, 5)); // 9 (5+2=7,
then add2(7)=9)
```

Explanation: `applyTwice` is a HOF since it takes fn as an argument.

Exercise 7: Partial Application Using a Returned Function

Task: Write a function `add(a)` that returns another function taking b and returning a+b.

Solution:

```javascript
function add(a) {
  return function(b) {
    return a + b;
  };
}
const add5 = add(5);
console.log(add5(10)); // 15
```

Explanation: add returns a function, making it higher-order.

Exercise 8: Implement a find Polyfill

Task: Write a myFind function that mimics find() using forEach().

Solution:

```javascript
function myFind(arr, predicate) {
  let found;
  arr.forEach(element => {
    if (found === undefined &&
predicate(element)) {
      found = element;
    }
  });
  return found;
}
console.log(myFind([1,2,3,4], x => x > 2)); // 3
```

Explanation: myFind takes a predicate function. forEach() is also a HOF.

Exercise 9: Compose Functions

Task: Write a compose(f,g) function that returns a new function
(x) => f(g(x)).

Solution:

```
function compose(f, g) {
  return function(x) {
    return f(g(x));
  };
}
function double(x) { return x * 2; }
function increment(x) { return x + 1; }
let doubleThenIncrement = compose(increment,
double);
console.log(doubleThenIncrement(5)); //
increment(double(5))= increment(10)=11
```

Explanation: compose returns a new function, making it a HOF.

Exercise 10: Chain Array Methods

Task: Given [1,2,3,4,5], use filter() and map() to first
filter out odd numbers and then double the even numbers.

Solution:

```
let data = [1,2,3,4,5];
let transformed = data
  .filter(num => num % 2 === 0)
  .map(num => num * 2);
console.log(transformed); // [4,8]
```

Explanation: Both `filter()` and `map()` are higher-order functions.

Summary

Higher-order functions are central to JavaScript's functional programming capabilities. By passing functions as arguments or returning them, you can create powerful abstractions, cleaner code, and reusable logic. Functions like `map`, `filter`, `reduce`, along with custom HOFs, enable flexible and expressive programming patterns.

Understanding Function Currying in JavaScript

What Is Currying?

Currying is a functional programming technique where a function that takes multiple arguments is transformed into a series of functions, each taking a single argument and returning a new function until all arguments have been provided.

For example, a function `f(a, b, c)` that takes three arguments can be turned into `f(a)(b)(c)`, where each invocation returns a new function waiting for the next argument. The final call, after receiving all arguments, returns the result.

Why Curry Functions?

1.   **Reusability & Modularity:**
Currying allows you to reuse functions with some arguments pre-applied and wait to receive the remaining arguments later.

2.   **Partial Application:**
Currying enables partial application — supplying some arguments now and the rest later, resulting in more flexible and composable code.

3.   **Functional Programming Style:**
Currying promotes a declarative and functional style, making logic more explicit and testable.

Currying vs Partial Application

●   **Currying** transforms a function of N arguments into N single-argument functions.

●   **Partial Application** is about applying some arguments now and returning a function that expects the remaining arguments. While closely related, partial application doesn't strictly require that the resulting function always takes one argument at a time; it can return a function still accepting multiple arguments.

Simple Currying Example

Without Currying:
```
function add(a, b) {
    return a + b;
}
```

```
console.log(add(2, 3)); // 5
```
With Currying:
```
function add(a) {
  return function(b) {
    return a + b;
  };
}
console.log(add(2)(3)); // 5
```

Curried Functions for More Arguments

For a function sum(a, b, c):
```
function sum(a, b, c) {
  return a + b + c;
}
// Curried version:
function sumCurry(a) {
  return function(b) {
    return function(c) {
      return a + b + c;
    };
  };
}
console.log(sumCurry(1)(2)(3)); // 6
```

Generic Currying Utility Function

We can write a utility to curry any function automatically:

```
function curry(fn) {
    return function curried(...args) {
        if (args.length >= fn.length) {
            // If enough arguments have been supplied
            return fn(...args);
        } else {
            // Otherwise, return a function expecting
the remaining arguments
            return function(...rest) {
                return curried(...args, ...rest);
            };
        }
    };
}
function multiply(a, b, c) {
    return a * b * c;
}
const curriedMultiply = curry(multiply);
console.log(curriedMultiply(2)(3)(4)); // 24
console.log(curriedMultiply(2,3)(4));  // 24
(partial application)
```

When to Use Currying?

- When you want to avoid passing the same argument multiple times.
- Creating specialized versions of a function for reuse.
- Making code more composable and functional.

Multiple-Choice Questions

1.   **What is currying?**

A. Cooking a function slowly.

B. Transforming a multi-argument function into a series of unary functions.

C. A method to call a function multiple times in a loop.

D. Converting an object into a function.

Answer: B

Explanation: Currying is about splitting a function taking multiple arguments into multiple functions taking one argument each.

2.   **Which is a curried form of f(a,b) = a+b?**

A. f(a)(b) = a+b

B. f(a,b,c)= a+b+c

C. f()() with no arguments

D. f(a,b)= a-b

Answer: A

Explanation: f(a)(b) is the curried form of a function taking two arguments.

3.   **Currying vs Partial Application:**

A. They are identical concepts.

B. Currying always returns unary functions, partial application doesn't have to.

C. Partial application requires all arguments at once.

D. Currying doesn't allow partial application.

Answer: B

Explanation: Curried functions return one-argument functions at each step. Partial application is more general.

4.   **If add is a curried function of 2 arguments, how do you call it?**

A. add(a,b)

B. add()(a)(b)

C. add(a)(b)

D. add([a,b])

Answer: C

Explanation: A 2-argument curried function is called as add(a)(b).

5.   **What does a curried function return when not all arguments are provided?**

A. The final result

B. A function waiting for the remaining arguments

C. undefined

D. An error

Answer: B

Explanation: A curried function returns a new function if it doesn't receive all arguments.

6.   **Currying makes it easier to:**

A. Change the arity (number of arguments) of a function at runtime.

B. Partially apply arguments for future use.

C. Directly call async functions.

D. Avoid closures.

Answer: B

Explanation: Currying naturally supports partial application of arguments.

7.　　**Given a curried function f(a)(b)(c), how many arguments does the original function take?**

A. 1

B. 2

C. 3

D. Unknown

Answer: C

Explanation: There are three successive calls, each taking one argument, so originally it took three arguments.

8.　　**If curry(fn) transforms fn, what must fn have?**

A. A known fixed arity (length)

B. Arbitrary arguments only

C. Always a single argument

D. No return value

Answer: A

Explanation: The curry utility typically uses fn.length to know how many arguments fn expects.

9.　　**Which of the following is a benefit of currying?**

A. Code becomes imperatively structured.

B. Functions become harder to reuse.

C. Simplifies function composition and reuse.

D. No difference in code clarity.

Answer: C

Explanation: Currying often leads to more composable and reusable code.

10. **In which programming paradigm is currying a common practice?**

A. Object-Oriented Programming

B. Functional Programming

C. Procedural Programming

D. Imperative Programming

Answer: B

Explanation: Currying is a common practice in functional programming.

11. **If a curried function takes 4 arguments, how many nested functions will it typically produce?**

A. 1

B. 2

C. 3

D. 4

Answer: D

Explanation: It produces a chain of 4 one-argument functions.

12. **What happens if you call a curried function with all its required arguments at once if the curry function supports partial application?**

A. It returns the final result immediately.

B. It returns another function.

C. It throws an error.

D. It returns undefined.

Answer: A

Explanation: If all required arguments are passed, the curried function returns the final result.

13. **A curried `multiply(2)(3)` equals:**

A. 2

B. 3

C. 6

D. A function expecting arguments

Answer: C

Explanation: `multiply` curried: `multiply(2)(3)` = 2 * 3 = 6.

14. **Currying a function that takes n arguments results in:**

A. A function that can only take one argument at a time until all are provided.

B. A single function that still requires n arguments at once.

C. A function that no longer requires arguments.

D. No change to the function's calling style.

Answer: A

Explanation: Currying transforms it into a sequence of unary functions.

15. **The `curry()` utility function often checks:**

A. `fn.name` property

B. `fn.length` property

C. `fn.toString()` result

D. `fn.constructor`

Answer: B

Explanation: `fn.length` gives the number of parameters fn expects, useful for deciding when all arguments are supplied.

16. **Which is true about currying and side effects?**

A. Currying requires no side effects for correctness.

B. Currying is unrelated to side effects; it's about argument handling.

C. Currying only works with pure functions.

D. Currying always introduces side effects.

Answer: B

Explanation: Currying doesn't mandate purity or side effects; it's about how arguments are supplied.

17. **Can you use arrow functions to create curried functions?**

A. Yes, arrow functions can also return functions.

B. No, you must use traditional function syntax.

C. Only with async functions.

D. Only if the function has one argument.

Answer: A

Explanation: Arrow functions can be used freely in curried functions.

18. **If a curried function needs more arguments than provided in the first call, it returns:**

A. An error

B. A partially applied function waiting for the rest of the arguments

C. The final result anyway

D. null

Answer: B

Explanation: The key idea of currying is returning a function waiting for the remaining arguments.

19. **What is the best scenario to apply currying?**

A. When you need to pass the same argument repeatedly to many functions.

B. When you only call a function once.

C. For CPU-intensive operations.

D. To handle exceptions.

Answer: A

Explanation: Currying helps reuse functions with some arguments fixed, useful if the same argument is needed repeatedly.

20. **Which is a valid curried calling style for a 3-argument function f?**

A. f(a,b,c)

B. f(a)(b)(c)

C. f(a)(b,c)

D. f([a,b,c])

Answer: B

Explanation: The standard curried form for a 3-argument function is f(a)(b)(c).

10 Coding Exercises with Full Solutions and Explanations

Exercise 1: Curried Addition

Task: Create a curried function add(a)(b) that returns a+b.

Solution:

```
function add(a) {
```

```
  return function(b) {
    return a + b;
  };
}
console.log(add(2)(3)); // 5
```

Explanation: Basic two-argument curried function.

Exercise 2: Curried Triple Argument Function

Task: Create a curried function sum(a)(b)(c) that returns a+b+c.

Solution:

```
function sum(a) {
  return function(b) {
    return function(c) {
      return a + b + c;
    };
  };
}
console.log(sum(1)(2)(3)); // 6
```

Explanation: Three nested functions, each taking one argument.

Exercise 3: Generic Curry Function

Task: Write a curry(fn) function that can curry a function with any number of arguments.

Solution:

```
function curry(fn) {
  return function curried(...args) {
    if (args.length >= fn.length) {
```

```
      return fn(...args);
    } else {
      return (...rest) => curried(...args,
...rest);
    }
  };
}
function multiply(a, b, c) {
  return a * b * c;
}
const curriedMultiply = curry(multiply);
console.log(curriedMultiply(2)(3)(4)); // 24
```

Explanation: Uses the function's `length` property and rest parameters to handle partial application.

Exercise 4: Using Curried Functions for Configuration

Task: Create a curried function `config(env)(debug)(port)` that returns an object `{env, debug, port}`.

Solution:

```
function config(env) {
  return function(debug) {
    return function(port) {
      return { env, debug, port };
    };
  };
}
```

```
console.log(config("production")(true)(8080));
// {env: "production", debug: true, port: 8080}
```
Explanation: Curried arguments to build a configuration object step by step.

Exercise 5: Partially Apply Arguments with Curry

Task: Given the curried sum from Exercise 2, create a partially applied version that always adds 10 first.

Solution:

```
const add10 = sum(10);
console.log(add10(5)(2)); // sum(10)(5)(2) = 17
```

Explanation: Using partial application, we fix a=10 and then only need two more calls.

Exercise 6: Curry a Function with curry() Utility

Task: Use the curry() function from Exercise 3 to curry a concat function that concatenates three strings.

Solution:

```
function concat(a, b, c) {
    return a + b + c;
}
const curriedConcat = curry(concat);
console.log(curriedConcat("Hello")("
")("World")); // "Hello World"
```

Explanation: curry() handles argument accumulation.

Exercise 7: Curried Filtering

Task: Create a curried function

`filterBy(predicate)(array)` that filters array by predicate.

Solution:

```
function filterBy(predicate) {
  return function(array) {
    return array.filter(predicate);
  };
}
const isEven = x => x % 2 === 0;
console.log(filterBy(isEven)([1,2,3,4])); //
[2,4]
```

Explanation: The first call sets the predicate, the second call filters the array.

Exercise 8: Curried Map

Task: Create a curried function `mapWith(fn)(array)` that maps array using fn.

Solution:

```
function mapWith(fn) {
  return function(array) {
    return array.map(fn);
  };
}
const double = x => x*2;
console.log(mapWith(double)([1,2,3])); // [2,4,6]
```

Explanation: Similar pattern to filtering, but with map.

Exercise 9: Reuse Curried Functions for Composability

Task: Use the `filterBy` and `mapWith` from previous exercises to first filter even numbers and then double them.

Solution:

```
console.log(mapWith(double)(filterBy(isEven)([1,2
,3,4,5,6]))); // [4,8,12]
```

Explanation: Curried functions allow piping:

`mapWith(double)(filterBy(isEven)(...))`.

Exercise 10: Curry a Preexisting Function

Task: Curry the built-in `Math.min` which takes multiple arguments, and try calling it as `curriedMin(5)(3)(2)`.

Note: `Math.min` can take multiple arguments, but we must consider a fixed number for demonstration. Let's assume we want a version that only compares three numbers.

Solution:

```
function curry(fn) {
    return function curried(...args) {
        if (args.length >= fn.length) {
            return fn(...args);
        } else {
            return (...rest) => curried(...args,
...rest);
        }
    };
}
// Let's create a 3-argument wrapper for Math.min
```

```
function min3(a, b, c) {
    return Math.min(a, b, c);
}
```

```
const curriedMin = curry(min3);
```

```
console.log(curriedMin(5)(3)(2)); // 2
```

Explanation: By currying a three-argument version of `Math.min`, we can call it in a curried style.

Summary

Currying is a powerful technique that transforms a function with multiple arguments into a nested series of one-argument functions. This approach enhances code reusability, composability, and clarity in functional programming. Through the exercises and examples given, you now have a solid understanding of how to implement and leverage currying in JavaScript, as well as a set of questions and answers to consolidate your knowledge.

Understanding Function Composition in JavaScript

What Is Function Composition?

Function composition is a functional programming technique where you combine multiple functions into a single function. The output of one function becomes the input of the next. Composing functions allows you to build complex transformations and logic by plugging together smaller, reusable functions.

For example, if you have two functions f and g, composing them $(f(g(x)))$ means you first apply g to x, then apply f to the result of $g(x)$.

Why Use Function Composition?

1.   **Reusability and Modularity:**
Compose small, single-responsibility functions to form more complex operations without rewriting code.

2.   **Readability:**
Complex operations are broken down into a chain of simpler steps, making the code more understandable.

3.   **Maintainability:**
Changing one part of the composed pipeline is easier since each function is independent.

Basic Composition Example

```
function addOne(x) {
   return x + 1;
}
function double(x) {
   return x * 2;
}
// Compose addOne and double: we want a function
that doubles then adds one
```

```javascript
function compose(f, g) {
  return function(x) {
    return f(g(x));
  };
}
```

```javascript
const addOneThenDouble = compose(double, addOne);
console.log(addOneThenDouble(3)); //
double(addOne(3)) = double(4) = 8
```

In the above code, `compose(double, addOne)` creates a new function: `(x) => double(addOne(x))`.

Composition Order Matters

- `compose(f, g)(x) = f(g(x))`

The function on the right (g) applies first, and the function on the left (f) applies second.

- If you reverse the order, `compose(g, f)(x) = g(f(x))`, which is often different.

Multiple Functions Composition

To compose more than two functions, you can nest them or write a compose function that takes multiple functions:

```javascript
function composeMany(...fns) {
  return function(x) {
```

```
    return fns.reduceRight((acc, fn) => fn(acc),
x);
  };
}
function addOne(x) { return x + 1; }
function double(x) { return x * 2; }
function square(x) { return x * x; }
const composed = composeMany(square, double,
addOne);
console.log(composed(2)); // (2 + 1) = 3,
double(3)=6, square(6)=36 but wait carefully:
order is right to left
// reduceRight applies rightmost first:
// start with x=2
// apply addOne(2) =3
// apply double(3)=6
// apply square(6)=36
```

Make sure the order is correct: `composeMany(square,`
`double, addOne)(2)` means apply `addOne` first, then `double`,
then `square`.

Pipe vs Compose

- **compose(...fns)** usually applies functions from right to left.
- **pipe(...fns)** applies functions from left to right.

```
function pipe(...fns) {
```

```
  return function(x) {
    return fns.reduce((acc, fn) => fn(acc), x);
  };
}
const piped = pipe(addOne, double, square);
console.log(piped(2)); // addOne(2)=3,
double(3)=6, square(6)=36
```

pipe is just a reversed composition—helpful for readability in some cases.

Real-World Scenarios

- **Data transformations:**
Compose functions that clean, transform, and validate data step by step.
- **String formatting:**
Compose functions that trim whitespace, change case, and add prefixes/suffixes.
- **Functional pipelines:**
Define your logic as a pipeline of transformations.

Multiple-Choice Questions

1. **What is function composition?**
A. Combining multiple functions to run in parallel.
B. Combining multiple functions so that the output of one is the input of the next.

C. Storing multiple functions in an array.

D. Reducing the number of arguments a function takes.

Answer: B

Explanation: Composition means chaining functions so the output of one feeds into the next.

2.   **Which of these examples shows function composition of f and g?**

A. f(g(x))

B. f + g

C. f * g

D. f | g

Answer: A

Explanation: Composition is typically represented as f(g(x)).

3.   **In a typical compose(f, g) function, which function is applied first to x?**

A. f first, then g

B. g first, then f

C. Both at the same time

D. Depends on the implementation

Answer: B

Explanation: compose(f, g)(x) = f(g(x)), g applies first.

4.   **Which function composition method applies functions from left to right?**

A. compose

B. pipe

C. Both compose and pipe

D. Neither

Answer: B

Explanation: Typically, `pipe` applies left to right, while `compose` applies right to left.

5.   **If we define compose(f, g) as x => f(g(x)), and we do compose(g, f)(x), what is the order of application?**

A. Still `f(g(x))`

B. `g(f(x))`

C. `f(x)(g(x))`

D. `f(x) + g(x)`

Answer: B

Explanation: `compose(g, f)` = x => `g(f(x))`, reversed order.

6.   **Why use function composition?**

A. To make code more complex

B. To combine large functions into monoliths

C. To build complex logic from simpler functions, improving reusability and clarity

D. It's a required syntax in ES6

Answer: C

Explanation: Composition improves code clarity and reusability.

7.   **composeMany(...fns) typically uses which array method to apply functions in order?**

A. `map`

B. `reduce` or `reduceRight`

C. `filter`

D. forEach

Answer: B

Explanation: `reduce` or `reduceRight` is often used to apply composed functions in the correct order.

8.   **Given f = x=>x+1 and g = x=>x*2, what is compose(f,g)(2)?**

A. `f(g(2))` = `f(4)=5`

B. `g(f(2))` = `g(3)=6`

C. 5 or 6 depending on how we define compose

D. Throws error

Answer: A

Explanation: With `compose(f,g)`, g runs first: g(2)=4, then f(4)=5.

9.   **If pipe(f,g)(x) is defined, which runs first?**

A. f first then g

B. g first then f

C. Both simultaneously

D. None

Answer: A

Explanation: `pipe(f,g)(x)` = g(f(x)), so f is applied first in a pipe scenario.

10.   **What is the difference between composition and currying?**

A. Currying transforms a function's arguments, composition chains functions.

B. Composition transforms arguments into multiple functions.

C. Currying and composition are identical.

D. Composition only works with arrays.

Answer: A

Explanation: Currying deals with argument structure, composition deals with chaining functions together.

11. **A composed function is:** A. Always pure

B. Always impure

C. Pure if the original functions are pure

D. Cannot be pure

Answer: C

Explanation: Composition preserves purity if all composed functions are pure.

12. **If compose is defined as compose(...fns), which order does it apply functions?**

A. Left to right

B. Right to left

C. Random order

D. Depends on the arguments

Answer: B

Explanation: By convention, compose applies functions from right to left.

13. **For composeMany(square, double, addOne)(2), what runs first if using reduceRight?**

A. square(2)

B. double(2)

C. addOne(2)

D. addOne is last, so it runs first: addOne(2)=3, then double(3)=6, then square(6)=36

Answer: D

Explanation: reduceRight starts from rightmost: addOne ->
double -> square.

14.   **If you have functions that rely on async operations,
can they still be composed in the same way?**

A. Yes, but you must handle promises or async patterns.

B. No, composition only works on synchronous functions.

C. Only if using `await`.

D. Only if converting all functions to strings.

Answer: A

Explanation: Async functions can be composed, but you must
handle async logic (e.g., returning promises, `pipeAsync`, etc.).

15.   **What is `pipe(addOne, double)(2)` if
`addOne=x=>x+1` and `double=x=>x*2`?**

A. `double(addOne(2))` = double(3)=6

B. `addOne(double(2))`=addOne(4)=5

C. 2

D. 3

Answer: A

Explanation: `pipe(addOne, double)` = x =>
double(addOne(x)), so addOne(2)=3, double(3)=6.

16.   **Function composition encourages:**

A. Large, monolithic functions

B. Small, reusable functions

C. Global variables

D. Mutation of state

Answer: B

Explanation: Composition works best with small, reusable functions.

17. If h = `compose(f,g)` and we do `h(x)`, what is returned?

A. `f(g(x))`

B. `g(f(x))`

C. `f(x)+g(x)`

D. Nothing

Answer: A

Explanation: By definition, `compose(f,g)(x)=f(g(x))`.

18. **Which pattern is the opposite of compose in terms of function order?**

A. `pipe`

B. `reduce`

C. `filter`

D. `map`

Answer: A

Explanation: `pipe` applies functions left to right, opposite of `compose`.

19. **When composing functions, what is the final argument we provide to the composed function?**

A. Another function

B. The initial input value

C. No arguments needed

D. A boolean

Answer: B

Explanation: Once composed, you provide an initial input to run through the chain.

20.   **If composeMany(...fns)(x) is called with no functions, what happens?**

A. Error

B. Returns x unchanged (identity)

C. Always returns undefined

D. Hangs the program

Answer: B

Explanation: With no functions, the composition is an identity function, returning x.

10 Coding Exercises with Full Solutions and Explanations

Exercise 1: Simple Compose

Task: Implement a compose function that takes two functions f and g and returns a new function (x) => f(g(x)).

Solution:

```
function compose(f, g) {
  return function(x) {
    return f(g(x));
  };
}
function addOne(x) { return x+1; }
function double(x) { return x*2; }
```

```
const composed = compose(double, addOne);
console.log(composed(3)); // double(addOne(3))=
double(4)=8
```
Explanation: Basic two-function composition.

Exercise 2: Compose Multiple Functions

Task: Create a composeMany(...fns) that composes any number of functions right-to-left.

Solution:
```
function composeMany(...fns) {
  return function(x) {
    return fns.reduceRight((acc, fn) => fn(acc),
x);
  };
}
function addOne(x) { return x+1; }
function double(x) { return x*2; }
function square(x) { return x*x; }
const multi = composeMany(square, double,
addOne);
console.log(multi(2)); // addOne(2)=3,
double(3)=6, square(6)=36
```
Explanation: Uses reduceRight to apply functions from right to left.

Exercise 3: Pipe Implementation

Task: Implement a pipe(...fns) function that applies functions left-to-right.

Solution:

```
function pipe(...fns) {
  return function(x) {
    return fns.reduce((acc, fn) => fn(acc), x);
  };
}
```

```
const pipeline = pipe(addOne, double, square);
console.log(pipeline(2)); // addOne(2)=3,
double(3)=6, square(6)=36
```

Explanation: Similar to compose, but using reduce left-to-right.

Exercise 4: Compose String Functions

Task: Create two functions `trim(str)` and `toUpperCase(str)`. Compose them so that given a string with extra spaces, you trim and then uppercase it.

Solution:

```
function trim(str) { return str.trim(); }
function toUpperCase(str) { return
str.toUpperCase(); }
```

```
const transform = compose(toUpperCase, trim);
console.log(transform("  hello world  ")); //
"HELLO WORLD"
```

Explanation: `compose(toUpperCase, trim)` means `toUpperCase(trim(str))`.

Exercise 5: Partial Composition with Known Functions

Task: Using composeMany, apply parseInt, then Math.abs, then addOne to a string number.

Solution:

```
function addOne(x) { return x+1; }
const chain = composeMany(addOne, Math.abs,
parseInt);
console.log(chain("-42")); // parseInt("-42")= -
42, Math.abs(-42)=42, addOne(42)=43
```

Explanation: The order is parseInt -> Math.abs -> addOne.

Exercise 6: Identity with Empty Composition

Task: Show that composeMany() with no functions just returns the input.

Solution:

```
const nothing = composeMany();
console.log(nothing(5)); // 5
```

Explanation: With no functions, reduceRight does nothing, just returns initial value.

Exercise 7: Reusable Functions in Composition

Task: Create increment(x), double(x) and decrement(x) and compose them to form a pipeline: increment -> double -> decrement.

Solution:

```
function increment(x) { return x+1; }
function double(x) { return x*2; }
function decrement(x) { return x-1; }
```

```
const pipeline = composeMany(decrement, double,
increment);
console.log(pipeline(5)); // increment(5)=6,
double(6)=12, decrement(12)=11
```

Explanation: Each step transforms the data in turn.

Exercise 8: Compose Array Methods

Task: Compose a function that first filters even numbers, then maps them to their squares.

Solution:

```
function filterEvens(arr) {
    return arr.filter(x => x % 2 === 0);
}
function squareAll(arr) {
    return arr.map(x => x*x);
}
const evenThenSquare = composeMany(squareAll,
filterEvens);
console.log(evenThenSquare([1,2,3,4,5,6])); //
filterEvens => [2,4,6], squareAll => [4,16,36]
```

Explanation: The composition ensures filter happens before map.

Exercise 9: Compose with Pipe

Task: Using pipe, create a pipeline that takes a number, increments, doubles, and logs the result.

(Assume a log function that logs and returns the value.)

Solution:

```
function log(x) { console.log(x); return x; }
```

```
const pipeline = pipe(increment, double, log);
pipeline(3); // increment(3)=4, double(4)=8,
log(8)=8 prints 8
```

Explanation: Pipe applies increment, then double, then log.

Exercise 10: Handling Errors in Composition

Task: Create two functions: `safeUpperCase(str)` which checks if `str` is a string, else returns it unchanged, and `exclaim(str)` which adds `!`. Compose them and test with a non-string.

Solution:

```
function safeUpperCase(str) {
   return typeof str === 'string' ?
str.toUpperCase() : str;
}
function exclaim(str) {
   return typeof str === 'string' ? str + '!' :
str;
}
const shout = composeMany(exclaim,
safeUpperCase);
console.log(shout("hello")); //
safeUpperCase("hello")="HELLO",
exclaim("HELLO")="HELLO!"
console.log(shout(123)); //
safeUpperCase(123)=123, exclaim(123)=123
```

Explanation: The composed function gracefully handles non-string input.

Summary

Function composition allows you to combine small, single-purpose functions into more complex operations, improving code clarity, testability, and reusability. By understanding and applying compose, pipe, and related techniques, you can write cleaner, more expressive JavaScript code. The included quiz and exercises provide a solid grounding in how to effectively use function composition in your projects.

Understanding `call()`, `apply()`, and `bind()` in JavaScript

What Are `call()`, `apply()`, and `bind()`?

`call()`, `apply()`, and `bind()` are methods available on all JavaScript functions. They allow you to explicitly set the `this` context for a function and, in the case of `call()` and `apply()`, also invoke the function with given arguments. `bind()` returns a new function with a permanently bound `this` and optionally preset arguments, without invoking it immediately.

Why Set this Explicitly?

In JavaScript, `this` can vary depending on how a function is called. Using `call()`, `apply()`, or `bind()`, you can precisely control `this`, enabling cleaner reuse of functions, borrowing methods from other objects, or ensuring a certain context for callback functions.

The Differences at a Glance

- **`call()`**:
  - Syntax: `func.call(thisArg, arg1, arg2, ...)`
  - Invokes the function immediately, allowing you to specify `this` and pass arguments individually.
- **`apply()`**:
  - Syntax: `func.apply(thisArg, [argArray])`
  - Similar to `call()`, but takes arguments as an array rather than individually.
- **`bind()`**:
  - Syntax: `const boundFunc = func.bind(thisArg, arg1, arg2, ...)`
  - Does not invoke the function immediately. Instead, returns a new function permanently bound to the specified `this` and pre-filled arguments if provided.

When to Use Each?

- Use **call()** when you know the arguments individually. E.g., `func.call(obj, x, y)`.
- Use **apply()** when you have arguments in an array or want to spread them easily. E.g., `func.apply(obj, [x, y])`.
- Use **bind()** when you want a new function with a fixed `this` context (and possibly some preset arguments) that you can call later. E.g., `const bound = func.bind(obj); bound(x, y);`

Common Use Cases

Method Borrowing:

```
const obj = { name: "Alice" };
function greet() {
   console.log("Hello, " + this.name);
}
greet.call(obj); // "Hello, Alice"
```

Max of an Array Using apply():

```
const numbers = [1,2,3];
const max = Math.max.apply(null, numbers); // 3
```

Currying / Partial Application with bind():

```
function add(a, b) {
   return a + b;
```

```
}
const addFive = add.bind(null, 5);
console.log(addFive(10)); // 15
```
Ensuring this in callbacks:

```
const module = {
  x: 42,
  getX: function() {
    return this.x;
  }
};
const unboundGetX = module.getX;
console.log(unboundGetX()); // undefined (because
`this` is global or undefined in strict mode)
const boundGetX = unboundGetX.bind(module);
console.log(boundGetX()); // 42
```

Multiple-Choice Questions

1.   **Which of the following methods invokes a function immediately while allowing you to specify the this value and arguments individually?**
A. `call()`
B. `apply()`
C. `bind()`

D. toString()

Answer: A

Explanation: call() invokes the function immediately with provided this and arguments listed individually.

2. **Which method is similar to call() but expects arguments as an array?**

A. bind()

B. apply()

C. callArray()

D. push()

Answer: B

Explanation: apply() is like call() but takes arguments in an array.

3. **What does bind() return?**

A. The return value of the function

B. A new function that can be called later with this bound

C. A boolean value

D. Undefined

Answer: B

Explanation: bind() returns a new function with this fixed, not immediately calling the original function.

Given:

```
const obj = { value: 10 };
function showValue() { console.log(this.value); }
showValue.call(obj);
```

4.   What is output?

A. `undefined`

B. `10`

C. `this.value` as a string

D. No output

Answer: B

Explanation: `showValue.call(obj)` sets `this` to `obj`, logging `10`.

5.   **If you have `Math.max.apply(null, [1,2,3])`, what is the result?**

A. 3

B. undefined

C. null

D. Error

Answer: A

Explanation: `apply()` calls `Math.max(1,2,3)`, returning 3.

6.   **What is the main difference between `call()` and `apply()`?**

A. `call()` doesn't allow `this` specification.

B. `apply()` doesn't invoke the function.

C. `call()` takes arguments individually, `apply()` takes arguments as an array.

D. They are identical in every way.

Answer: C

Explanation: The key difference is how arguments are passed.

7. **What does `bind()` do if you pass arguments along with this?**

A. It sets up partial application, so those arguments are preset for future calls.

B. It ignores extra arguments.

C. It immediately invokes the function.

D. It throws an error.

Answer: A

Explanation: `bind()` can preset arguments, creating a partially applied function.

8. **Which method would you use to borrow a method from one object and use it on another object immediately?**

A. `bind()`

B. `call()`

C. `apply()`

D. new

Answer: B or C

Explanation: Both `call()` and `apply()` can do this immediately, but since the question says "immediately" and individually passing arguments, `call()` is a more direct fit. However, `apply()` also works if arguments are in an array. The safest answer is B (`call()`) since it's commonly used for immediate invocation.

9. **If `func.bind(obj)` is called, does it invoke `func` immediately?**

A. Yes

B. No, it returns a new function to call later

C. Sometimes

D. Only if `obj` is null

Answer: B

Explanation: `bind()` never immediately invokes the function.

Consider:

```javascript
const person = {
  name: "Alice",
  greet: function(greeting) {
    console.log(greeting + ", " + this.name);
  }
};
const greetBob = person.greet.bind({ name: "Bob" }, "Hello");
greetBob();
```

10.   What is logged?

A. "Hello, Bob"

B. "Hello, Alice"

C. Error: `this.name` is undefined

D. "Hello, [object Object]"

Answer: A

Explanation: `bind()` sets `this` to `{ name: "Bob" }` and presets "Hello" as an argument.

11.   **`apply()` is often used for which common trick?**

A. Converting array-like objects into arrays using `Array.prototype.slice.apply(...)`

B. Creating classes

C. Immediately calling a constructor

D. Blocking scope

Answer: A

Explanation: `apply()` is famously used for method borrowing from `Array.prototype` on array-likes.

12. **If you have `func.call(obj, 1, 2)` and `func.apply(obj, [1,2])`, do they produce the same result?**

A. Yes, assuming `func` and `obj` are the same

B. No, the results differ

C. `apply()` is slower

D. `call()` is asynchronous

Answer: A

Explanation: The only difference is how arguments are passed, but the result is the same.

13. **Can you change the `this` of an arrow function using `call` or `apply`?**

A. Yes, arrow functions respect `call()` and `apply()`

B. No, arrow functions' `this` is lexically bound and cannot be changed

C. Only with `bind()`

D. Only in strict mode

Answer: B

Explanation: Arrow functions have lexical `this` and ignore `call`, `apply`, `bind` for `this` changes.

14. **If bind() is used on a function multiple times with different this values, what happens?**

A. The last bind overrides previous ones

B. The first bind is permanent; subsequent binds are ignored

C. It throws an error

D. Functions cannot be bound more than once

Answer: B

Explanation: Once a function is bound, rebinding it doesn't change its this.

15. **When would you use bind() over call()?**

A. If you want to invoke immediately

B. If you want a new function you can call later with the same this

C. If you have arguments in an array format

D. Never; bind and call are the same

Answer: B

Explanation: bind() creates a new function, useful for later calls.

16. **What is the value of this if you do func.call(null, 1,2) in non-strict mode?**

A. this becomes null strictly

B. this defaults to the global object (window in browsers)

C. Throws an error

D. this is always undefined

Answer: B

Explanation: In non-strict mode, passing `null` or `undefined` to `call()` makes `this` the global object.

17.   **What is a common use-case for `bind()` in event handlers?**

A. To set the event target as `this`

B. To ensure a class method keeps its `this` when used as a callback

C. To immediately invoke a handler

D. To copy the event object

Answer: B

Explanation: `bind()` is often used so that methods retain their class instance `this` in callbacks.

18.   **Does `bind()` permanently change the original function?**

A. Yes

B. No, it returns a new function and doesn't alter the original

C. It depends on the function type

D. Only if the function is in strict mode

Answer: B

Explanation: `bind()` creates a new bound function without modifying the original function.

19.   **`func.apply(thisArg, argumentsArray)` requires what type for the arguments?**

A. A plain object

B. A string

C. An array or array-like object

D. No arguments allowed

Answer: C

Explanation: `apply()` expects the second argument to be an array or array-like.

20.   **If a function returns `this`, what can happen if you use `bind()`?**

A. `this` will still refer to the bound object.

B. `this` is lost

C. The return value changes

D. Throws error

Answer: A

Explanation: If the function returns `this`, after binding, `this` is the bound context, so it returns that context.

10 Coding Exercises with Full Solutions and Explanations

Exercise 1: Using `call()` to Borrow a Method

Task: You have an object `person` with a `greet()` method and another object `dog` without it. Use `call()` to make `dog` use `person`'s greet method.

Solution:

```
const person = {
  name: "Alice",
  greet: function(greeting) {
    console.log(greeting + ", " + this.name);
```

```
  }
};
const dog = { name: "Fido" };
person.greet.call(dog, "Woof"); // "Woof, Fido"
```
Explanation: `call()` sets this to dog.

Exercise 2: Using apply() with a Built-in Function

Task: Use `apply()` to find the maximum value in an array `[10, 20, 3]` using `Math.max`.

Solution:
```
const arr = [10,20,3];
const max = Math.max.apply(null, arr);
console.log(max); // 20
```
Explanation: `apply()` passes `arr` as arguments to `Math.max`.

Exercise 3: Using bind() to Fix this in a Callback

Task: Fix the `this` context in a callback function by using `bind()`.

Solution:
```
const module = {
  x: 42,
  getX: function() { return this.x; }
};
const unbound = module.getX;
console.log(unbound()); // undefined, `this` lost
const bound = unbound.bind(module);
console.log(bound()); // 42
```

Explanation: `bind()` ensures `this` is always `module` when `bound` is called.

Exercise 4: Partial Application with `bind()`

Task: Create a function `add(a,b)` and use `bind()` to create `addTen` that always adds 10.

Solution:

```
function add(a, b) {
   return a + b;
}
const addTen = add.bind(null, 10);
console.log(addTen(5)); // 15
```

Explanation: `bind()` sets the first argument a=10 permanently.

Exercise 5: Using `call()` with Varying Arguments

Task: Create a function that logs all arguments it receives. Use `call()` to pass arguments individually.

Solution:

```
function logArgs() {
   console.log([...arguments].join(', '));
}
logArgs.call(null, 'apple', 'banana', 'cherry');
// "apple, banana, cherry"
```

Explanation: `call()` allows passing arguments individually.

Exercise 6: Using `apply()` to Convert Array-like Objects

Task: Use `apply()` on `Array.prototype.slice` to convert `arguments` of a function into a real array.

Solution:

```
function toArray() {
    return Array.prototype.slice.apply(arguments);
}
console.log(toArray(1,2,3)); // [1,2,3]
```

Explanation: apply() calls slice with arguments as if it were an array.

Exercise 7: Multiple bind() Calls

Task: Bind a function to one object, then try to bind the result to another object. Verify which this is used.

Solution:

```
function showName() { console.log(this.name); }
const obj1 = { name: "Obj1" };
const obj2 = { name: "Obj2" };
const boundToObj1 = showName.bind(obj1);
const boundToObj2 = boundToObj1.bind(obj2);
boundToObj2(); // "Obj1", not "Obj2"
```

Explanation: The first bind is permanent.

Exercise 8: Using apply() with No Arguments

Task: Call a function that takes multiple arguments with apply() but pass an empty array.

Solution:

```
function greet(name) {
    return "Hello, " + name;
}
```

```
console.log(greet.apply(null, ["Alice"])); //
"Hello, Alice"
console.log(greet.apply(null, [])); // "Hello,
undefined" (no argument provided)
```

Explanation: `apply()` can take an empty array if no arguments needed.

Exercise 9: Borrowing `join` Method Using `call()`

Task: Borrow `Array.prototype.join` to join arguments of a function into a string separated by -.

Solution:

```
function joinWithDash() {
  return Array.prototype.join.call(arguments, '-
');
}
console.log(joinWithDash("red", "green",
"blue")); // "red-green-blue"
```

Explanation: `call()` sets this to `arguments` so `join` treats it as an array.

Exercise 10: Ensure Method Works As Expected in Another Context Using `bind()`

Task: You have a method `increment()` in one object. Create a bound version that always increments a specific object's property.

Solution:

```
const counter = {
  value: 0,
```

```
  increment: function() { this.value++; }
};
const incrementCounter =
counter.increment.bind(counter);
incrementCounter();
console.log(counter.value); // 1
const anotherCounter = { value: 100 };
const incrementAnother =
counter.increment.bind(anotherCounter);
incrementAnother();
console.log(anotherCounter.value); // 101
```
Explanation: Each bind creates a new function tied to a specific object.

Summary

-     `call()` and `apply()` both invoke a function immediately, differing only in how arguments are provided (individually vs. array).
-     `bind()` returns a new function with a permanently set `this`, allowing you to control the function's context later.
-     They enable flexible code reuse, function borrowing, partial application, and maintainable event handlers and callbacks.

Understanding Recursive Functions in JavaScript

What Is a Recursive Function?

A recursive function is a function that calls itself, either directly or indirectly. Instead of looping constructs, recursion uses repeated function calls to break down problems into smaller and more manageable pieces. Each recursive call reduces the complexity of the problem until it reaches a base case, a simple condition that stops the recursion.

Key Concepts

1. **Base Case:**
A condition that when met, stops the recursive calls. Without a proper base case, a recursive function can cause infinite recursion.
2. **Recursive Case:**
The part of the function that reduces the problem size and calls itself with the new, smaller problem.

Classic Examples

Factorial using recursion:

```
function factorial(n) {
    if (n === 0) {
```

```
    return 1; // base case
  }
  return n * factorial(n - 1); // recursive case
}
console.log(factorial(5)); // 120
```

Fibonacci numbers using recursion:

```
function fibonacci(n) {
  if (n <= 1) {
    return n; // base cases fib(0)=0, fib(1)=1
  }
  return fibonacci(n-1) + fibonacci(n-2);
}
console.log(fibonacci(6)); // 8 (sequence:
0,1,1,2,3,5,8)
```

Sum of an array recursively:

```
function sumArray(arr, index=0) {
  if (index === arr.length) {
    return 0; // base case: no more elements
  }
  return arr[index] + sumArray(arr, index+1); //
recursive step
}
console.log(sumArray([1,2,3,4])); // 10
```

Benefits of Recursion

- Can simplify code for problems naturally described by smaller subproblems.
- Useful for tree/graph traversal, mathematical computations (factorial, Fibonacci), and divide-and-conquer algorithms (merge sort, quicksort).

Potential Pitfalls

- Without a proper base case, recursion leads to infinite loops.
- Deep recursion can cause stack overflow errors.
- Sometimes recursion is less efficient than iterative solutions due to repeated computations and function call overhead.

Tail Recursion (Not Natively Optimized in JS)

Tail recursion is a form of recursion where the recursive call is the last statement in the function. Some languages optimize tail calls to prevent stack growth, but JavaScript does not reliably do so (as of current ECMAScript standards).

Converting Recursive to Iterative

Most recursive functions can be converted into iterative solutions using loops or stacks. Whether to use recursion or iteration depends on readability, performance needs, and problem nature.

Multiple-Choice Questions

1.   **What is recursion?**

A. A function calling another unrelated function.

B. A function calling itself.

C. A loop that never ends.

D. A function that takes no arguments.

Answer: B

Explanation: Recursion is when a function calls itself.

2.   **Which of the following is essential for a recursive function?**

A. A global variable.

B. A base case.

C. An if-else statement.

D. Strict mode.

Answer: B

Explanation: A base case prevents infinite recursion.

3.   **What happens if a recursive function has no base case?**

A. It stops after one call.

B. It results in infinite recursion and eventually a stack overflow.

C. It returns 0 by default.

D. It throws a syntax error.

Answer: B

Explanation: Without a base case, recursion never ends.

4.   **Which example shows a correct recursive call in factorial calculation?**

A. `return factorial(n);`

B. `return n * factorial(n-1);`

C. `return factorial(n+1);`

D. `return factorial(0);`

Answer: B

Explanation: For factorial: `factorial(n) = n * factorial(n-1)` until the base case.

5.   **If `fibonacci(0)=0` and `fibonacci(1)=1`, how is `fibonacci(n)` defined recursively for n>1?**

A. `fibonacci(n) = fibonacci(n)`

B. `fibonacci(n) = fibonacci(n-2)`

C. `fibonacci(n) = fibonacci(n-1) + fibonacci(n-2)`

D. `fibonacci(n) = n`

Answer: C

Explanation: The Fibonacci sequence is fib(n)=fib(n-1)+fib(n-2) for n>1.

6.   **What can happen if recursion is too deep?**

A. Nothing special, it always works.

B. It can cause a stack overflow error.

C. It switches to an iterative mode automatically.

D. It returns null.

Answer: B

Explanation: Extremely deep recursion can exceed call stack limits.

7.   **Which is often easier to implement using recursion?**

A. Iterating over a simple array.

B. Traversing a tree structure.

C. Calculating simple arithmetic sums.

D. Printing a fixed message.

Answer: B

Explanation: Recursive functions naturally model hierarchical structures like trees.

8.   **What is tail recursion?**

A. Recursion that occurs at the start of a function.

B. Recursion with multiple base cases.

C. A form of recursion where the recursive call is the last thing the function does.

D. Recursion that doesn't use arguments.

Answer: C

Explanation: Tail recursion is when the recursive call is the final statement.

9.   **Does JavaScript currently optimize tail recursion?**

A. Yes, always.

B. Only in strict mode.

C. Only in older browsers.

D. Not reliably in current ECMAScript standards.

Answer: D

Explanation: Tail call optimization is not reliably implemented in modern JavaScript engines.

10.   **Converting recursion to iteration often involves using what data structure?**

A. Arrays only

B. A stack or a queue

C. A global variable

D. A random number generator

Answer: B

Explanation: Recursion can be mimicked iteratively using a stack or queue.

11. **Which of the following is a base case in a recursive sum of array function?**

A. When `index === arr.length`

B. When `arr` is always non-empty

C. When `arr` has negative numbers

D. When `arr` is sorted

Answer: A

Explanation: When you've reached the end of the array, you return 0 as the base case.

12. **What is a disadvantage of recursion?**

A. It always runs faster than iteration.

B. It can be less memory-efficient and cause stack overflow if not careful.

C. It simplifies all problems.

D. It's impossible to debug.

Answer: B

Explanation: Recursion can lead to more memory usage and potential stack overflow.

Which function best showcases a correct approach for factorial(3)?

```
function factorial(n) {
  if (n === 0) return 1;
  return n * factorial(n-1);
}
```

13.   A. This is correct

B. Missing base case

C. Wrong calculation

D. Should use a loop instead

Answer: A

Explanation: This is the standard recursive definition for factorial.

14.   **For a function that prints a countdown from n to 1 using recursion, what could be the base case?**

A. When n < 1

B. When n is always positive

C. No base case needed

D. When n is even

Answer: A

Explanation: Once n < 1, no more printing is needed.

15.   **A recursive function to compute the length of a linked list uses what base case?**

A. When the next node is null (end of list)

B. When the head is always non-null

C. When a cycle is detected

D. Linked lists don't use recursion

Answer: A

Explanation: When you hit a null reference (end of the list), return 0.

16.   **When would you prefer recursion over iteration?**

A. When dealing with hierarchical or tree-like data structures, or when it makes the solution more understandable.

B. Always, because recursion is faster.

C. Never, iteration is always better.

D. Only in non-strict mode

Answer: A

Explanation: Use recursion when it clarifies the solution for complex hierarchical problems.

17. **If a recursive function calls itself twice per invocation (like fibonacci), what is the complexity?**

A. O(n) always

B. Potentially exponential (like O(2^n))

C. O(log n)

D. O(1)

Answer: B

Explanation: Two recursive calls per invocation often lead to exponential growth, like naive Fibonacci.

18. **What could be a reason to convert a recursive function to iterative?**

A. To reduce memory usage and avoid stack overflow.

B. Because recursion is not allowed in JS.

C. Iteration is always shorter to write.

D. Functions cannot return values when recursive.

Answer: A

Explanation: Iteration might be more efficient and safer for large input.

19. **Is it possible for a recursive function to call itself indirectly through another function?**

A. Yes, indirect recursion occurs when function A calls function B which calls function A.

B. No, recursion must be direct.

C. Only if in strict mode.

D. Only with arrow functions.

Answer: A

Explanation: Indirect recursion is still recursion: A calls B, B calls A.

20.   **Which statement is true about recursion and debugging?**

A. Recursion makes debugging impossible.

B. Debugging recursion may be more challenging, but it's still possible using call stacks.

C. Recursion does not appear in call stacks.

D. Recursion hides errors.

Answer: B

Explanation: Debugging is possible, but can be more complex since you must track many calls in the stack.

10 Coding Exercises with Full Solutions and Explanations

Exercise 1: Factorial

Task: Write a recursive function `factorial(n)` that returns n! for n≥0.

Solution:
```
function factorial(n) {
  if (n === 0) return 1;
  return n * factorial(n - 1);
}
```

```
console.log(factorial(5)); // 120
```

Explanation: Base case: factorial(0)=1. Recursive step: factorial(n)=n*factorial(n-1).

Exercise 2: Fibonacci

Task: Write a recursive function `fibonacci(n)` returning the nth Fibonacci number.

Solution:

```
function fibonacci(n) {
  if (n <= 1) return n;
  return fibonacci(n - 1) + fibonacci(n - 2);
}
console.log(fibonacci(6)); // 8
```

Explanation: Base cases: fib(0)=0, fib(1)=1. Recursive step: fib(n)=fib(n-1)+fib(n-2).

Exercise 3: Sum of Array

Task: Implement `sumArray(arr)` that sums all elements using recursion.

Solution:

```
function sumArray(arr, index=0) {
  if (index === arr.length) return 0;
  return arr[index] + sumArray(arr, index + 1);
}
console.log(sumArray([1,2,3,4])); // 10
```

Explanation: Base case: when index=arr.length, return 0. Recursive step: add current element and recurse.

Exercise 4: Count Down

Task: Write `countDown(n)` that prints numbers from n down to 1 using recursion.

Solution:

```
function countDown(n) {
    if (n < 1) return;
    console.log(n);
    countDown(n-1);
}
countDown(5);
// prints 5,4,3,2,1
```

Explanation: Base case: if n<1, stop. Otherwise print n and recurse with n-1.

Exercise 5: Reverse a String

Task: Implement `reverseString(str)` recursively.

Solution:

```
function reverseString(str) {
    if (str.length <= 1) return str;
    return reverseString(str.slice(1)) +
str.charAt(0);
}
console.log(reverseString("hello")); // "olleh"
```

Explanation: Base case: length ≤1 means return the string.

Recursive step: reverse substring and append first char.

Exercise 6: Power Function

Task: Write power(base, exponent) recursively.

Solution:

```
function power(base, exponent) {
    if (exponent === 0) return 1;
    return base * power(base, exponent - 1);
}
console.log(power(2,3)); // 8
```

Explanation: Base case: exponent=0 → return 1. Recursive: base

* power(base, exp-1).

Exercise 7: Check Palindrome

Task: isPalindrome(str) returns true if str is palindrome, else false.

Solution:

```
function isPalindrome(str) {
    if (str.length <= 1) return true;
    if (str[0] !== str[str.length - 1]) return
false;
    return isPalindrome(str.slice(1, -1));
}
console.log(isPalindrome("racecar")); // true
console.log(isPalindrome("hello"));   // false
```

Explanation: Base: length ≤1 → true. Check first and last char, if

same, recurse on middle substring.

Exercise 8: Sum of Digits

Task: Given a number, return the sum of its digits recursively.

Solution:

```
function sumDigits(num) {
  const str = num.toString();
  if (str.length === 1) return parseInt(str);
  return parseInt(str[0]) +
sumDigits(parseInt(str.slice(1)));
}
console.log(sumDigits(1234)); // 1+2+3+4=10
```

Explanation: Base: single digit, return it. Otherwise add first digit and recurse on remainder.

Exercise 9: Depth of Nested Arrays

Task: arrayDepth(arr) returns the maximum depth of nested arrays.

Solution:

```
function arrayDepth(arr) {
  if (!Array.isArray(arr)) return 0;
  let max = 1;
  for (let item of arr) {
    if (Array.isArray(item)) {
      max = Math.max(max, 1 + arrayDepth(item));
    }
  }
  return max;
}
```

```
console.log(arrayDepth([1,[2,[3]]])); // 3
```
Explanation: Base: if not array, depth=0. Otherwise check each item, if array, depth=1+ depth(item).

Exercise 10: Binary Search with Recursion

Task: Implement `binarySearch(arr, target)` recursively, assuming `arr` is sorted.

Solution:
```
function binarySearch(arr, target, left=0,
right=arr.length-1) {
  if (left > right) return -1; // base case: not
found
  const mid = Math.floor((left+right)/2);
  if (arr[mid] === target) return mid;
  if (target < arr[mid]) {
    return binarySearch(arr, target, left, mid-
1);
  } else {
    return binarySearch(arr, target, mid+1,
right);
  }
}
console.log(binarySearch([1,2,3,4,5,6],4)); // 3
(0-based index)
```
Explanation: Base case: if left>right, not found. Otherwise check mid and recurse into left or right half.

Summary

Recursive functions are powerful tools in JavaScript that let you solve problems by breaking them down into smaller pieces. Properly identified base cases prevent infinite recursion, and careful design can make complex problems easier to understand. While recursion can be elegant, consider performance and the risk of stack overflow for large inputs. The exercises and questions provided should give you solid foundational knowledge and hands-on practice with recursive functions in JavaScript.

Understanding Pure Functions in JavaScript

What Are Pure Functions?

A **pure function** is a function that, given the same inputs, always returns the same output and does not produce any observable side effects. In other words, pure functions:

1.   Do not depend on or modify any external state (no side effects).

2.   Always return the same result given the same arguments (referential transparency).

Characteristics of Pure Functions

1. **No Side Effects:**

A pure function cannot alter variables outside its scope, mutate its arguments, perform I/O operations, or modify global state.

2. **Deterministic:**

A pure function's output depends solely on its input arguments. If you call it multiple times with the same arguments, you get the same result.

3. **Easier to Test and Reason About:**

Because pure functions do not rely on external state, they are simpler to test. Just pass arguments and check the return value.

Examples of Pure vs. Impure Functions

Pure Function Example:

```
function add(a, b) {
   return a + b; // Returns a value solely derived
from input arguments
}
```

Impure Function Example:

```
let counter = 0;
function incrementCounter() {
   counter++; // modifies external variable, thus
causing side effects
   return counter;
}
```

More Pure Examples:

```
function square(x) {
```

```
    return x * x; // no side effects, purely
depends on x
}
function concatStrings(a, b) {
    return a + b; // no external state modified, no
side effects
}
```

Impure Due to Mutation:

```
function pushToArray(arr, value) {
    arr.push(value); // mutates external array
    return arr;
}
```

This is not pure because it changes the original array. A pure version would return a new array:

```
function addToArray(arr, value) {
    return [...arr, value]; // returns a new array,
doesn't mutate arr
}
```

Benefits of Pure Functions

- Easier testing: No need for mocks or complicated setups.
- Predictability: Given inputs, you always know the output.
- Facilitates functional programming patterns like composition and memoization.

Avoiding Side Effects

To keep functions pure, avoid:

- Mutating external variables.
- Performing I/O (like DOM manipulation, network requests, console logs).
- Using `this` in a way that depends on external state.

Pure Functions in Functional Programming

In functional programming, most logic is built upon pure functions. Data transformations become more predictable and composable.

Multiple-Choice Questions

1. **What is a pure function?**

A. A function that never returns anything.

B. A function that always produces the same output for the same input and has no side effects.

C. A function that uses global variables.

D. A function that relies on random numbers.

Answer: B

Explanation: A pure function has no side effects and is deterministic.

2. **Which of the following is a side effect?**

A. Returning a computed value.

B. Logging to the console.

C. Using only local variables.

D. Adding two numbers.

Answer: B

Explanation: Logging to the console is an observable side effect.

3.   **If a function mutates an object passed as an argument, is it pure?**

A. Yes, arguments are fair game to change.

B. No, mutating arguments is a side effect.

C. Only if the object is global.

D. Only if it returns the same object.

Answer: B

Explanation: Mutating arguments is considered a side effect.

Which of the following is a pure function?

```
let x = 10;
function f(y) {
    return x + y;
}
```

4.   A. Yes, it's pure.

B. No, it depends on external variable x.

C. Yes, because it returns something.

D. No, because it returns a sum.

Answer: B

Explanation: It depends on x which is external state.

5.   **A pure function always:**

A. Returns the same result given the same inputs.

B. Logs errors if something fails.

C. Manipulates the DOM.

D. Calls this inside.

Answer: A

Explanation: Determinism is a key property of pure functions.

6.   **What is not an example of a side effect?**

A. Changing a global variable.

B. Modifying a parameter object.

C. Reading a global variable without changing it.

D. Writing to the console.

Answer: C

Explanation: Reading global state is generally considered a mild impurity, but the strict definition of pure function often excludes reading from external variables. For a strict definition, let's say reading from global state can also be considered a side effect. However, reading global constants might be allowed if they never change. The best answer here given the options is C, because reading (not modifying) global variables is often considered less severe. But purest definition says even reading a changing global variable breaks purity. The question is tricky. Among given options, changing global var is a clear side effect, modifying parameter is side effect, writing to console is side effect. Reading global variable—some consider it pure if it's a constant. We'll consider reading global state as a subtle impurity. The question says "What is not an example of a side effect?" The least side-effect-likely is reading global variable. Let's stick with C.

7.   **If a function uses Math.random(), is it pure?**

A. Yes, always.

B. No, because output changes each time.

C. Yes, if it returns the random value.

D. Only if seeded.

Answer: B

Explanation: `Math.random()` makes outputs vary, breaking referential transparency.

8.   **Which property do pure functions support that helps in caching results?**

A. Idempotency

B. Memoization

C. Mutation

D. Overloading

Answer: B

Explanation: Because pure functions always return same output for same input, they can be memoized.

9.   **Is returning a new array inside a function considered a side effect?**

A. Yes, returning new arrays is always a side effect.

B. No, returning a new value is not a side effect.

C. Only if the array is modified globally.

D. Only if the array is empty.

Answer: B

Explanation: Returning new data is not a side effect. Side effect = external change.

10.   **A pure function cannot:**

A. Be reused.

B. Be tested easily.

C. Depend on changing global variables.

D. Return objects.

Answer: C

Explanation: Pure functions must not depend on changing external states.

11.   **Pure functions in functional programming help with:**

A. Harder debugging.

B. Unpredictable code.

C. Easier reasoning and testing.

D. More side effects.

Answer: C

Explanation: Pure functions make reasoning and testing simpler.

Which is an example of a pure function?

```
function multiply(a, b) {
   return a * b;
}
```

12.   A. Pure

B. Impure (depends on external state)

C. Impure (no return)

D. Impure (mutates arguments)

Answer: A

Explanation: `multiply(a, b)` just returns a*b, no side effects.

13.   **Can pure functions modify their arguments?**

A. Yes, if they return a value.

B. Yes, if arguments are primitive.

C. No, modifying arguments is a side effect.

D. Only in strict mode.

Answer: C

Explanation: Changing arguments mutates external data passed in.

14. **Are pure functions allowed to call other pure functions?**

A. Yes, composing pure functions is encouraged.

B. No, calls to other functions are side effects.

C. Only if they log results.

D. Only if they use bind.

Answer: A

Explanation: Composition of pure functions remains pure.

15. **If a pure function throws an error given certain input, is it still pure?**

A. Yes, it's still pure as long as it has no side effects.

B. No, throwing an error is a side effect.

C. Only if error is caught.

D. Only if error is logged.

Answer: A

Explanation: Throwing an error is not a side effect; it's a predictable outcome for that input.

16. **Pure functions and referential transparency means:**

A. You can replace a function call with its output if inputs are known.

B. You must always use loops.

C. You cannot return strings.

D. The function must be async.

Answer: A

Explanation: Referential transparency means function calls can be replaced with their result.

17. **What if a function reads a global constant that never changes?**

A. Still considered impure by most strict definitions.

B. It can be considered pure if that global never changes, acting like a constant.

C. Always impure.

D. Depends on ES version.

Answer: B

Explanation: If global is truly constant and unchanging, it's effectively pure. Some strict definitions might still argue it's impure, but commonly accepted as pure.

18. **Is writing to a file a side effect?**

A. No, it's just output.

B. Yes, I/O is a side effect.

C. Only if the file is global.

D. Not if the same content is written every time.

Answer: B

Explanation: Any I/O is considered a side effect.

19. **Can pure functions be used in memoization?**

A. Yes, perfectly, since inputs map to outputs deterministically.

B. No, because results vary.

C. Only if they mutate arguments.

D. Only if they have side effects.

Answer: A

Explanation: Pure functions are ideal for memoization.

20. **What best describes a pure function's advantage in parallel execution?**

A. They cannot be run in parallel.

B. Pure functions are thread-safe since no external state is changed.

C. They cause race conditions.

D. They require locks.

Answer: B

Explanation: Pure functions are thread-safe and can be executed in parallel without race conditions.

10 Coding Exercises with Full Solutions and Explanations

Exercise 1: Simple Pure Function Task: Create a pure function add(a, b) that returns a+b.

Solution:

```
function add(a, b) {
   return a + b; // purely depends on inputs
}
console.log(add(2,3)); // 5
```

Explanation: No external state, no side effects, always same result for same inputs.

Exercise 2: Convert Impure to Pure Task: You have:

```
let count = 0;
function increment() {
   count++;
   return count;
}
```

Make it pure.

Solution:

```
function incrementPure(value) {
    return value + 1;
}
console.log(incrementPure(5)); // 6, doesn't rely
on external variable
```

Explanation: Now it takes an input and returns incremented result without modifying outside state.

Exercise 3: Pure Concatenation Task: Write `concatStrings(a, b)` that returns a+b without using global variables.

Solution:

```
function concatStrings(a, b) {
    return a + b;
}
console.log(concatStrings("Hello", "World")); //
"HelloWorld"
```

Explanation: No side effects, output depends only on inputs.

Exercise 4: Pure Array Append Task: Given an array and a value, return a new array with value appended, without mutating the original.

Solution:

```
function appendValue(arr, value) {
    return [...arr, value];
}
const original = [1,2];
const newArr = appendValue(original, 3);
```

```
console.log(original); // [1,2] unchanged
console.log(newArr);   // [1,2,3]
```
Explanation: Returns a new array, no mutation, pure function.

Exercise 5: Pure Square Function Task: square(x) returns x*x purely.

Solution:
```
function square(x) {
   return x * x;
}
console.log(square(4)); //16
```
Explanation: Trivial pure function.

Exercise 6: Pure Filter Task: Given an array and a predicate, return a new filtered array (like a mini filter function), without mutating original.

Solution:
```
function pureFilter(arr, predicate) {
   let result = [];
   for (let item of arr) {
     if (predicate(item)) {
        result = [...result, item];
     }
   }
   return result;
}
console.log(pureFilter([1,2,3,4], x => x%2===0));
// [2,4]
```

Explanation: Returns a new array, no mutation, depends only on inputs and the predicate.

Exercise 7: Pure Increment by a Constant Task: Create `incrementBy(n, incrementValue)` that returns n+incrementValue.

Solution:

```
function incrementBy(n, incrementValue) {
    return n + incrementValue;
}
console.log(incrementBy(10,5)); //15
```

Explanation: Pure, no side effects.

Exercise 8: Pure Maximum Task: Write `max(a, b)` that returns the larger of two numbers.

Solution:

```
function max(a, b) {
    return a > b ? a : b;
}
console.log(max(3,7)); //7
```

Explanation: Pure function, depends solely on inputs.

Exercise 9: Pure Reverse String Task: Given a string, return its reverse without changing external state or using console.

Solution:

```
function reverseString(str) {
    return str.split('').reverse().join('');
}
console.log(reverseString("abc")); // "cba"
```

Explanation: Creates new string from input, no side effects.

Exercise 10: Pure Average Calculation Task: Write `average(nums)` that returns the average of an array of numbers purely.

Solution:

```
function average(nums) {
  if (nums.length === 0) return 0;
  const sum = nums.reduce((acc, val) => acc +
val, 0);
  return sum / nums.length;
}
console.log(average([1,2,3,4])); // 2.5
```

Explanation: Does not mutate anything, just calculates and returns result.

Summary

Pure functions are a cornerstone of functional programming, making code more predictable, testable, and composable. They always return the same output for the same input, have no side effects, and do not rely on external state. By practicing writing pure functions, developers can produce cleaner, more maintainable code.

Understanding Arrow Functions in JavaScript

What Are Arrow Functions?

Arrow functions (introduced in ES6) provide a more concise syntax for writing functions. They are defined using the => syntax, have implicit returns in simple cases, and do not bind their own this context, arguments, or super. Instead, they inherit this from the parent (lexical scope).

Basic Syntax

Traditional function:

```
function add(a, b) {
    return a + b;
}
```

Arrow function equivalent:

```
const add = (a, b) => {
    return a + b;
};
// With implicit return (if just one expression):
const addShort = (a, b) => a + b;
```

Key Features of Arrow Functions

1.   **Concise Syntax:**
○   If there's a single parameter, parentheses around parameters can be omitted.

```
const square = x => x * x;
```

- If there's a single expression in the function body, braces and `return` can be omitted, returning that expression implicitly.

No Own this:

Arrow functions do not have their own `this`. Instead, `this` is taken from the lexical scope. This means `this` inside an arrow function is the same as `this` in the outer context.

Example:

```
const obj = {
  value: 10,
  regularFunc: function() {
    console.log(this.value); // 10
  },
  arrowFunc: () => {
    console.log(this.value); // undefined,
because 'this' is from global scope in strict
mode
  }
};
obj.regularFunc(); // 10
obj.arrowFunc();   // undefined
```

2. To properly use `this` in arrow functions that need context, define the arrow function inside a method or a constructor where `this` is already what you want it to be.

3.   **No arguments Object:**

Arrow functions do not have an `arguments` object. To access parameters, you must use rest parameters (`...args`) if needed.

4.   **Cannot be used as constructors:**

Arrow functions cannot be used with `new` because they don't have a `[[Construct]]` method. They are not suitable as constructor functions.

5.   **No prototype Property:**

Arrow functions don't have a prototype property since they're not meant for use as constructors.

Common Use Cases

●   Arrow functions shine in callbacks, array methods (`map`, `filter`, `reduce`), and event listeners, providing concise code.

●   They are great for situations where you want lexical `this` binding and avoid writing `.bind(this)`.

Examples:

Implicit return with one argument:

```
const double = x => x * 2;
console.log(double(5)); // 10
```

No this binding:

```
function Person() {
  this.age = 0;
  // Using arrow function, 'this' refers to
Person instance, no bind needed.
```

```
setInterval(() => {
    this.age++;
    console.log(this.age);
}, 1000);
}
new Person();
```

As callback in array methods:

```
const numbers = [1,2,3];
const squares = numbers.map(n => n*n);
console.log(squares); // [1,4,9]
```

Multiple-Choice Questions

1.   **What is an arrow function?**

A. A new syntax for classes

B. A shorter syntax for writing function expressions

C. A method to create objects

D. The only way to declare functions

Answer: B

Explanation: Arrow functions provide a concise way to write function expressions.

2.   **Which of the following correctly defines an arrow function that adds two numbers?**

A. `const add = (a, b) => { return a + b; }`

B. `const add = => (a,b) a + b;`

C. `const add (a,b) => a+b;`

D. add = a, b => a + b;

Answer: A

Explanation: (a,b) => {return a+b;} is correct syntax. Also (a,b) => a+b works.

3. **When can you omit parentheses around parameters in an arrow function?**

A. When there are no parameters

B. When there is exactly one parameter

C. When there are two parameters

D. Never

Answer: B

Explanation: One parameter allows omitting parentheses, e.g. x => x*x.

4. **What about this in arrow functions?**

A. Arrow functions have their own this

B. this in arrow functions refers to global object always

C. Arrow functions do not bind their own this; they inherit it from lexical scope

D. this is always undefined in arrow functions

Answer: C

5. **Can arrow functions be used as constructors with new keyword?**

A. Yes, if you specify parameters

B. No, arrow functions cannot be constructed

C. Only in strict mode

D. Only if they return an object

Answer: B

Explanation: Arrow functions can't be used as constructors.

6.   **What is the implicit return in arrow functions?**

A. If there's a single expression without braces, that expression's value is returned automatically

B. Arrow functions never return a value unless explicitly stated

C. They always return undefined

D. Implicit return doesn't exist

Answer: A

7.   **Do arrow functions have an `arguments` object?**

A. Yes, same as regular functions

B. No, arrow functions do not have `arguments`

C. Only if in strict mode

D. Depends on how they are defined

Answer: B

8.   **Which is a valid arrow function with no parameters that returns "Hello"?**

A. `const greet = => "Hello";`

B. `const greet = () => "Hello";`

C. `const greet = () => { "Hello" }`

D. `const greet => "Hello";`

Answer: B

Explanation: `() => "Hello"` is correct syntax for no-parameter arrow function.

9.   **If an arrow function body has braces { }, what must you do to return a value?**

A. Nothing, it returns automatically

B. Use `return` statement inside the braces

C. You cannot return if braces are used

D. It's a syntax error to have braces

Answer: B

Explanation: With braces, you must explicitly return.

10.   **Can arrow functions access `this` from their outer lexical context?**

A. No, `this` is always undefined

B. Yes, they use lexical `this`

C. Yes, but must use .bind()

D. They generate a runtime error if `this` used

Answer: B

11.   **What happens if you try to use `arguments` inside an arrow function?**

A. It refers to the parent's arguments if any

B. It's undefined

C. Creates a reference error

D. It's a syntax error

Answer: A

Explanation: `arguments` is not defined in arrow function, they use outer scope or result in error if not defined. If there's no arguments in outer scope, referencing `arguments` would lead to error.

Which is shorter syntax for:

```
const multiply = function(a) { return a*2; }
```

12.   A. `const multiply = a => a*2;`

B. `const multiply = (a) => { a*2 }`

C. `const multiply = (a) => return a*2;`

D. `const multiply = => a*2;`

Answer: A

13.   **Do arrow functions have their own `this` binding?**

A. Yes, always points to window

B. No, `this` is taken lexically from parent scope

C. They do if used with new

D. They only have `this` in strict mode

Answer: B

14.   **Arrow functions and `.prototype`:**

A. Arrow functions have a prototype property

B. Arrow functions do not have a prototype property

C. They have prototype but it's always empty

D. prototype is always null

Answer: B

15.   **If you do `const fn = () => {}; new fn();` what happens?**

A. Creates a new object from fn

B. Throws a TypeError

C. Returns undefined

D. Works as normal function

Answer: B

Explanation: Arrow functions can't be used as constructors.

16.   **Arrow functions vs normal functions for object methods:**

A. Arrow functions are best for object methods to access `this`

B. Normal functions are better if you need `this` referring to object

C. No difference

D. Arrow functions always have correct `this`

Answer: B

Explanation: For object methods needing `this` of the object, normal functions are better because arrow `this` might not be what you expect.

17.   **Can arrow functions be named or are they always anonymous?**

A. They can be named by assigning to a variable

B. They must be anonymous

C. There's a name property but no direct naming syntax

D. They must have a name parameter

Answer: A

Explanation: Typically arrow functions are anonymous, but you can give them an identifier by assigning them to a variable.

18.   **If you want a method on a class to have `this` as class instance, arrow function vs normal method?**

A. Use arrow function if you want lexical `this` from class definition

B. Use normal method to get class instance `this`

C. Both behave identically in classes

D. Arrow functions in class fields get `this` from instance, normal methods from prototype

Answer: D

Explanation: Class field arrow functions capture `this` at instance creation time. Normal methods on the prototype have `this` determined by caller.

19. **Implicit return works when:**

A. Body is a single expression without braces

B. Always, regardless of braces

C. Only if you type `return`

D. In async arrow functions only

Answer: A

20. **To return an object literal implicitly, you must:**

A. Just write `{ key: value }`

B. Wrap object literal in parentheses: `() => ({key: value})`

C. It's impossible to return object implicitly

D. Add `return` keyword

Answer: B

Explanation: Without parentheses, `{}` is interpreted as block, so use `() => ({object})`.

10 Coding Exercises with Full Solutions and Explanations

Exercise 1: Basic Arrow Function

Task: Convert a function `add` into an arrow function with implicit return.

Solution:

```
const add = (a, b) => a + b;
console.log(add(2,3)); // 5
```

Explanation: Omitting `return` since single expression.

Exercise 2: Single Parameter Arrow

Task: Create an arrow function `square` that takes one param `x` and returns x*x.

Solution:

```
const square = x => x*x;
console.log(square(4)); // 16
```

Explanation: Single parameter: no parentheses needed.

Exercise 3: No Parameter Arrow

Task: Create an arrow function `hello` that returns "Hello World" with no parameters.

Solution:

```
const hello = () => "Hello World";
console.log(hello()); // "Hello World"
```

Explanation: No parameters: use `()`.

Exercise 4: Using `this` inside arrow

Task: Demonstrate `this` lexical binding by using arrow in a constructor.

Solution:

```
function Person(name) {
  this.name = name;
  // arrow inherits 'this' from Person scope
  this.sayName = () => console.log(this.name);
```

```
}
const p = new Person("Alice");
p.sayName(); // "Alice"
```
Explanation: this in arrow is Person instance, no bind needed.

Exercise 5: Trying to use arrow as constructor

Task: Show that new with arrow function throws error.

Solution:
```
const Arrow = () => {};
try {
  new Arrow(); // error
} catch(e) {
  console.log("Error using arrow as
constructor:", e.message);
}
```
Explanation: Using new on arrow results in TypeError.

Exercise 6: Returning object implicitly

Task: Return an object {a:1, b:2} implicitly from an arrow function.

Solution:
```
const getObject = () => ({ a:1, b:2 });
console.log(getObject()); // {a:1, b:2}
```
Explanation: Parentheses needed to avoid block interpretation.

Exercise 7: Arrow function in array methods

Task: Use arrow function in `.map()` to double array elements.

Solution:

```
const arr = [1,2,3];
const doubled = arr.map(x => x*2);
console.log(doubled); // [2,4,6]
```

Explanation: Arrow used as concise callback.

Exercise 8: Arrow function without arguments object

Task: Try to access `arguments` in arrow function and show alternative.

Solution:

```
// arrow doesn't have arguments
const arrowArgs = () => {
  try {
    console.log(arguments);
  } catch(e) {
    console.log("No arguments in arrow!");
  }
};
// Alternative using rest parameters
const arrowRest = (...args) => console.log(args);
arrowArgs(1,2,3); // "No arguments in arrow!"
```

```
arrowRest(1,2,3); // [1,2,3]
```

Explanation: `arguments` not available, use rest `...args`
instead.

Exercise 9: Arrow function in event listener

Task: Add a click listener using arrow function that logs `this` and
verify `this` is not the element.

Solution (in browser environment):
```
const btn = document.getElementById('myButton');
btn.addEventListener('click', () => {
  console.log("this inside arrow:", this); //
likely undefined or window
});
```
Explanation: `this` not bound to `btn`. For `this` as element, use
normal function.

Exercise 10: Leading to confusion - arrow vs normal function

Task: Show difference between arrow and normal function in
object method when accessing `this`.

Solution:
```
const obj = {
  val: 42,
  normalMethod: function() {
```

```
    console.log("normalMethod this.val:",
this.val); // 42
  },
  arrowMethod: () => {
    console.log("arrowMethod this.val:",
this.val); // undefined or error
  }
};
obj.normalMethod();
obj.arrowMethod();
```

Explanation: normalMethod has this = obj, arrowMethod this from lexical scope (probably global), not obj.

Summary

Arrow functions:

- Provide shorter syntax.
- Have lexical this, no own this or arguments.
- Can't be constructors, no prototype.
- Great for concise callbacks, array operations, and preserving this context from outer scope.
- Implicit return simplifies code when one expression is used.

Understanding Asynchronous JavaScript

What Is Asynchronous JavaScript?

JavaScript is single-threaded and executes code in a non-blocking manner. Instead of waiting for long-running operations (like network requests or file I/O) to complete, JavaScript continues executing the rest of the code. Once the operation completes, the result is handled asynchronously through callbacks, promises, or async/await.

The Event Loop

The event loop is a key concept:
- **Call Stack:** Executes synchronous code line by line.
- **Web APIs / Node APIs:** Handle asynchronous tasks, timers, and network requests.
- **Task Queue / Microtask Queue:** When async operations finish, their callbacks or promise handlers are placed into queues. The event loop then pushes these queued callbacks back to the call stack when it's free, allowing asynchronous code to run after synchronous code finishes.

Callback Functions

Initially, async in JavaScript was handled via callbacks:

```
setTimeout(() => {
  console.log("After 1 second");
}, 1000);
```

However, callback chains can become "callback hell" due to nested callbacks.

Promises

Promises provide a cleaner way to handle async operations:

```
fetch("https://api.example.com/data")
  .then(response => response.json())
  .then(data => console.log(data))
  .catch(error => console.error(error));
```

A promise represents a value that may be available now, later, or never. It can be in three states: pending, fulfilled, or rejected.

Async/Await

`async/await` syntax allows writing asynchronous code in a synchronous style:

```
async function fetchData() {
  try {
    const response = await
fetch("https://api.example.com/data");
    const data = await response.json();
    console.log(data);
  } catch (e) {
    console.error(e);
  }
}
fetchData();
```

`await` can only be used inside `async` functions, and it pauses the function execution until the promise resolves or rejects.

Microtasks vs. Macrotasks

- **Macrotasks:** setTimeout, setInterval, I/O tasks. Placed in the task queue.
- **Microtasks:** Promise callbacks (then/catch/finally). Placed in the microtask queue. The event loop handles microtasks before macrotasks when the call stack is empty.

Code Examples

Callback Example:

```
function doAsyncTask(callback) {
  setTimeout(() => {
    callback("Task complete");
  }, 500);
}
doAsyncTask(result => {
  console.log(result); // "Task complete"
});
```

Promise Example:

```
function asyncOp() {
  return new Promise((resolve, reject) => {
    setTimeout(() => resolve("Done"), 1000);
  });
```

```
}
asyncOp().then(value => console.log(value));
```

Async/Await Example:

```
async function main() {
  const value = await asyncOp();
  console.log(value); // "Done"
}
main();
```

Promise.all Example:

```
const p1 = Promise.resolve(1);
const p2 = Promise.resolve(2);
const p3 = Promise.resolve(3);
Promise.all([p1, p2, p3]).then(values => {
  console.log(values); // [1,2,3]
});
```

Multiple-Choice Questions

1.   **What is the purpose of the event loop in JavaScript?**

A. To execute code line by line synchronously.

B. To handle asynchronous operations by checking queues and pushing callbacks onto the call stack.

C. To increase performance by running multiple threads.

D. To parse JavaScript code.

Answer: B

Explanation: The event loop checks queues for async callbacks and runs them when the stack is clear.

2. **Which of these is not a way to handle async operations in JS?**

A. Callbacks

B. Promises

C. Async/Await

D. Synchronous loops

Answer: D

Explanation: Synchronous loops don't handle async; they block.

3. **In a callback-based async function, what causes "callback hell"?**

A. Using console.log too often.

B. Nested callbacks leading to deeply indented and hard-to-maintain code.

C. Too few callbacks.

D. Using arrow functions.

Answer: B

Explanation: Nested callbacks create complex, difficult-to-read code, known as callback hell.

4. **What are the possible states of a Promise?**

A. pending, settled

B. pending, fulfilled, rejected

C. started, stopped, paused

D. open, closed

Answer: B

Explanation: Promises start as pending and can either fulfill or reject.

5. **What does `fetch()` return?**

A. A Promise that resolves to a Response object.

B. A Callback function.

C. A synchronous object.

D. Nothing.

Answer: A

Explanation: fetch() returns a promise resolving to a Response.

6. **async function always returns what?**

A. A promise.

B. A callback.

C. An object.

D. Undefined.

Answer: A

Explanation: async functions return a promise.

7. **What does `await` do inside an async function?**

A. Stops the function completely.

B. Pauses execution until the promise settles.

C. Throws an error if promise rejects.

D. Executes code synchronously.

Answer: B

Explanation: `await` pauses the async function until promise resolves or rejects.

8. **If a promise is rejected and no `.catch()` is used, what happens?**

A. Nothing, silent failure.

B. Unhandled promise rejection warning/error.

C. The program crashes immediately.

D. The promise turns fulfilled.

Answer: B

Explanation: Unhandled rejections may cause warnings and potential errors.

9. **Which runs first when the call stack is empty, microtasks or macrotasks?**

A. Macrotasks first, then microtasks.

B. Microtasks first (like promise callbacks), then macrotasks.

C. Both run simultaneously.

D. They never run after stack is empty.

Answer: B

Explanation: Microtasks (promises) run before macrotasks (setTimeout).

10. **Promise.all([...]) does what?**

A. Runs promises sequentially.

B. Resolves when all promises fulfill, or rejects if one rejects.

C. Returns immediately with an array of unresolved promises.

D. Only works with callbacks.

Answer: B

Explanation: Promise.all waits for all to fulfill or rejects on first rejection.

11. **Which is not an asynchronous method in JS?**

A. setTimeout

B. fetch

C. Promise.then

D. JSON.parse

Answer: D

Explanation: JSON.parse is synchronous.

12. **If an async function throws an error, how do you handle it?**

A. With try/catch inside the async function.

B. You cannot handle it.

C. With a callback.

D. Using `await` outside.

Answer: A

Explanation: Errors in async/await can be handled with try/catch.

13. **Which is a recommended way to avoid callback hell?**

A. Use nested setTimeouts.

B. Use Promises or async/await.

C. Use more callbacks.

D. Avoid asynchronous code.

Answer: B

Explanation: Promises and async/await improve readability.

14. **What does `Promise.race(promises)` do?**

A. Resolves when the first promise resolves or rejects.

B. Resolves only if all resolve.

C. Rejects if all reject.

D. Calls a callback when done.

Answer: A

Explanation: Promise.race settles as soon as the first promise settles.

15. **Can `await` be used outside of an async function?**

A. Yes, in modern browsers with top-level await in modules.

B. No, never.

C. Yes, in any global script.

D. Only in Node.js.

Answer: A

Explanation: Historically no, but top-level await in ES modules is now allowed in modern environments. Without top-level await, must be inside async function.

16.   **If a promise is already fulfilled when `await` is used, what happens?**

A. `await` still pauses.

B. `await` returns the fulfilled value immediately without pausing.

C. `await` rejects.

D. `await` causes error.

Answer: B

Explanation: If promise is already resolved, `await` returns immediately.

17.   **What is `Promise.finally()` used for?**

A. To handle success only.

B. To handle rejections only.

C. To run code after resolve or reject, regardless of outcome.

D. To convert promise to async function.

Answer: C

Explanation: finally runs after promise settles, success or error.

18.   **How do you handle multiple async steps in sequence using async/await?**

A. Use multiple await statements in order.

B. Use Promise.race.

C. Use nested callbacks again.

D. Not possible.

Answer: A

Explanation: Await each promise in sequence with multiple awaits.

19.   **If a promise never resolves or rejects, what happens?**

A. The code after `.then()` is blocked forever.

B. The promise stays pending indefinitely.

C. It automatically rejects after some time.

D. The event loop stops.

Answer: B

Explanation: Promise stays pending, never settling.

20.   **Which queue are promise .then() handlers placed into?**

A. Macrotask queue.

B. Microtask queue.

C. Rendering queue.

D. Stack directly.

Answer: B

Explanation: Promise callbacks go into the microtask queue.

10 Coding Exercises with Full Solutions and Explanations

Exercise 1: Callback Basics

Task: Create a function `doTaskAsync(callback)` that uses `setTimeout` to call `callback("done")` after 500ms.

Solution:

```
function doTaskAsync(callback) {
  setTimeout(() => {
    callback("done");
```

```
  }, 500);
}
doTaskAsync(result => console.log(result)); //
"done" after 0.5s
```

Explanation: This shows basic callback-based async.

Exercise 2: Promise from Scratch

Task: Write a function delay(ms) that returns a Promise that resolves after ms milliseconds.

Solution:

```
function delay(ms) {
  return new Promise(resolve => {
    setTimeout(() => resolve(`Waited ${ms}ms`),
ms);
  });
}
delay(1000).then(msg => console.log(msg)); //
"Waited 1000ms" after 1s
```

Explanation: Creates a promise that resolves after a delay.

Exercise 3: Async/Await with Fetch

Task: Fetch JSON data from a public API using async/await and log the result.

Solution:

(Assuming a working API and a browser environment)

```
async function fetchData() {
```

```
  const response = await
fetch('https://jsonplaceholder.typicode.com/todos
/1');
  const data = await response.json();
  console.log(data);
}
fetchData();
```

Explanation: Uses await to pause until fetch and json are done, then logs result.

Exercise 4: Handling Errors with Try/Catch

Task: Write an async function that fetches from an invalid URL and catches the error.

Solution:

```
async function fetchInvalid() {
  try {
    const response = await
fetch('https://invalid.url');
    const data = await response.json();
    console.log(data);
  } catch (err) {
    console.error("Fetch error:", err);
  }
}
fetchInvalid();
```

Explanation: Errors are caught with try/catch in async function.

Exercise 5: Promise.all for Parallel Fetches

Task: Use `Promise.all` to fetch multiple endpoints in parallel and log all results.

Solution:

```
async function fetchMultiple() {
  const urls = [

'https://jsonplaceholder.typicode.com/todos/1',

'https://jsonplaceholder.typicode.com/todos/2'
  ];
  const promises = urls.map(url =>
fetch(url).then(r => r.json()));
  const results = await Promise.all(promises);
  console.log(results);
}
fetchMultiple();
```

Explanation: Promise.all waits for all fetches, then logs both results.

Exercise 6: Sequential Async Operations

Task: Perform two fetch calls in sequence using async/await.

Solution:

```
async function fetchSequential() {
  const response1 = await
fetch('https://jsonplaceholder.typicode.com/todos
/1');
```

```javascript
  const data1 = await response1.json();
  console.log("First:", data1);
  const response2 = await
fetch('https://jsonplaceholder.typicode.com/todos
/2');
  const data2 = await response2.json();
  console.log("Second:", data2);
}
fetchSequential();
```

Explanation: Each await waits for one operation before starting the next.

Exercise 7: Race Condition with Promise.race

Task: Use Promise.race with two promises: one resolves in 1s, another in 500ms. Log the first to finish.

Solution:

```javascript
function fastTask() {
  return new Promise(resolve => setTimeout(() =>
resolve("fast"), 500));
}
function slowTask() {
  return new Promise(resolve => setTimeout(() =>
resolve("slow"), 1000));
}
```

```
Promise.race([fastTask(),
slowTask()]).then(result => console.log(result));
// "fast"
```

Explanation: Promise.race resolves with the first settled promise.

Exercise 8: Converting Callback to Promise

Task: Given a callback style readFile(file, cb) function, wrap it in a function readFilePromise(file) that returns a promise.

Solution:

(Simulating readFile with setTimeout)

```
function readFile(file, cb) {
  setTimeout(() => {
    cb(null, "file content");
  }, 300);
}
function readFilePromise(file) {
  return new Promise((resolve, reject) => {
    readFile(file, (err, data) => {
      if (err) reject(err);
      else resolve(data);
    });
  });
}
readFilePromise("myfile.txt").then(content =>
console.log(content)); // "file content"
```

Explanation: Promisify a callback function by returning a new Promise.

Exercise 9: Using finally in Promise

Task: After a promise resolves, use `.finally()` to log "done".

Solution:

```
function asyncOp() {
    return new Promise(resolve => setTimeout(() =>
resolve("result"), 500));
}
asyncOp()
    .then(res => console.log(res))
    .finally(() => console.log("done"));
```

Explanation: finally runs after the promise is settled, no matter what.

Exercise 10: Microtask vs Macrotask Check

Task: Demonstrate that a promise then runs before a setTimeout callback by logging the order.

Solution:

```
console.log("Start");
Promise.resolve().then(() => console.log("Promise
then"));
setTimeout(() => console.log("setTimeout"), 0);
console.log("End");
// Order: "Start", "End", "Promise then",
"setTimeout"
```

Explanation: The promise `then` (microtask) runs before the `setTimeout` (macrotask).

Summary

Asynchronous JavaScript handles long-running tasks without blocking the main thread. The event loop, callbacks, promises, and async/await provide various patterns to handle async operations. Modern code often uses promises or async/await for clarity and maintainability. Mastery of these concepts is essential for building responsive and performant JavaScript applications.

Understanding the Event Loop, Task Queue, and Microtask Queue

The JavaScript Event Loop

JavaScript runs on a single thread, meaning only one piece of code executes at a time. The event loop is a mechanism that manages the execution of synchronous and asynchronous code, ensuring that non-blocking operations (like I/O, timers, promises) can be handled efficiently.

Task Queue (Macrotask Queue)

Task queue (often referred to as macrotask queue) holds tasks scheduled by functions like `setTimeout()`, `setInterval()`, `setImmediate()` (in Node.js), or I/O events. These tasks are larger units of work executed after the currently executing script and all microtasks complete.

- Examples of tasks (macrotasks):
  - `setTimeout(callback, 0)`
  - `setInterval(callback, time)`
  - I/O callbacks (e.g., `XMLHttpRequest` load event)

After the current stack finishes, the event loop checks the microtask queue first. If empty, it takes the next task from the task queue, pushes it onto the call stack, and executes it.

Microtask Queue

Microtask queue holds microtasks, which are smaller, more immediate callbacks. Microtasks are processed as soon as the current call stack is empty, **before** moving on to the next macrotask.

- Examples of microtasks:
  - Promises `.then()` and `.catch()` callbacks
  - `MutationObserver` callbacks
  - `queueMicrotask()` function

When the current JavaScript execution stack completes, the event loop first processes all microtasks in the microtask queue before picking the next macrotask from the task queue.

The Order of Execution

1. Execute the current script (synchronous code).

2.   When the call stack is empty, check the microtask queue:

○   If there are microtasks, run all of them until the microtask queue is empty.

3.   If no more microtasks, take the next task from the task (macrotask) queue and run it.

4.   Repeat.

Key Differences

●   **Microtasks** (in microtask queue):

○   Executed immediately after the currently running script finishes, before rendering and before any next macrotask.

○   Include promise callbacks, `queueMicrotask()`, `MutationObserver` callbacks.

●   **Tasks (Macrotasks)** (in task queue):

○   Executed after microtasks are cleared.

○   Include `setTimeout`, `setInterval`, I/O events.

Code Example Demonstrating Order

```
console.log("Start");
setTimeout(() => {
  console.log("Macrotask (setTimeout)");
}, 0);
Promise.resolve().then(() => {
  console.log("Microtask (Promise then)");
});
console.log("End");
```

```
// Order of logs:
// Start
// End
// Microtask (Promise then)
// Macrotask (setTimeout)
```
Here, Promise.then callback (microtask) runs before the setTimeout callback (macrotask).

Multiple-Choice Questions

1. **Which queue is processed first when the current call stack is empty?**

A. Task queue

B. Microtask queue

C. Both simultaneously

D. Whichever has fewer tasks

Answer: B

Explanation: Microtasks run before the next macrotask.

2. **A setTimeout callback goes into which queue?**

A. Microtask queue

B. Task (macrotask) queue

C. Directly on the call stack

D. It doesn't get queued

Answer: B

Explanation: setTimeout schedules a macrotask.

3. **Which of the following is a microtask source?**

A. setInterval

B. Promises `.then()`

C. XMLHttpRequest load event

D. `setTimeout`

Answer: B

Explanation: Promise `.then()` callbacks go to the microtask queue.

4.   **When does the event loop run microtasks?**

A. After each macrotask finishes and the call stack is empty.

B. Only once at the start of the script.

C. Before the synchronous code executes.

D. After all macrotasks complete.

Answer: A

Explanation: Microtasks are processed immediately after the current stack is empty, before the next macrotask.

5.   **If you have both a microtask and a macrotask ready, which runs first?**

A. Macrotask first

B. Microtask first

C. Whichever was queued first

D. Random order

Answer: B

Explanation: Microtasks have higher priority and run before macrotasks.

6.   **What is the main advantage of microtasks over macrotasks in JavaScript?**

A. They always run faster.

B. They allow code to run immediately after the current stack, improving responsiveness.

C. They skip error handling.

D. They run in parallel.

Answer: B

Explanation: Microtasks run sooner, right after current tasks finish, allowing more fine-grained asynchronous operations.

7. **Which function can be used to schedule a microtask explicitly?**

A. `queueMicrotask()`

B. `setImmediate()`

C. `setTimeout()`

D. `requestAnimationFrame()`

Answer: A

Explanation: `queueMicrotask()` adds a function to the microtask queue.

8. **If multiple `.then()` handlers are queued, in what order do they run?**

A. In the order they were queued, all in the microtask phase.

B. Random order.

C. After all macrotasks run.

D. They run synchronously.

Answer: A

Explanation: Multiple promise `.then()` callbacks enqueue in the microtask queue and run in order.

9. **Which is true about tasks (macrotasks)?**

A. They run before the main script.

B. They are run after microtasks are cleared.

C. They preempt currently running code.

D. They replace the event loop.

Answer: B

Explanation: Macrotasks run after all microtasks have finished.

10.   `Promise.resolve().then(...)` **callback goes into which queue?**

A. Macrotask queue

B. Microtask queue

C. Stack directly

D. Not queued at all

Answer: B

Explanation: `.then()` callbacks enter the microtask queue.

11.   **If you** `setTimeout(fn, 0)` **and also** `Promise.resolve().then(fn2)`**, which runs first?**

A. `fn` from setTimeout

B. `fn2` from promise `.then()`

C. They run simultaneously

D. Depends on browser

Answer: B

Explanation: The promise `.then()` (microtask) runs before the macrotask (setTimeout).

12.   **What happens if a microtask itself queues another microtask?**

A. The event loop runs that new microtask immediately after finishing the current round.

B. It goes to the macrotask queue.

C. It's ignored.

D. It runs before finishing the current microtask.

Answer: A

Explanation: Once the current microtask finishes, the event loop checks microtasks again, running newly added ones before macrotasks.

13.   **When is the DOM updated in relation to microtasks and macrotasks?**

A. After all microtasks but before the next macrotask

B. Before microtasks run

C. Right after each line of code

D. DOM updates occur only after macrotask.

Answer: A

Explanation: Typically, the browser updates the rendering after microtasks finish and before handling the next macrotask.

14.   **Is process.nextTick() in Node.js considered a microtask or macrotask?**

A. Macrotask

B. Microtask

C. Not a task at all

D. It's synchronous

Answer: B (In Node.js, process.nextTick() puts the callback into the microtask queue.)

15.   **Do microtasks interrupt currently running code?**

A. Yes, they run immediately

B. No, they run after the current execution stack finishes.

C. They can run at any time.

D. They run before the current code.

Answer: B

Explanation: Microtasks run after the current stack is empty.

16.   **What is a macrotask example besides setTimeout?**

A. Promise callbacks

B. setInterval callbacks

C. queueMicrotask tasks

D. .then() handlers

Answer: B

Explanation: setInterval also schedules macrotasks.

17.   **If no microtasks are queued, the event loop:**

A. Executes the next macrotask

B. Stops running

C. Throws an error

D. Forces a GC

Answer: A

Explanation: If no microtasks, event loop proceeds to next macrotask.

18.   **Microtasks were introduced to:**

A. Slow down async code

B. Provide more granular scheduling than macrotasks

C. Replace setTimeout

D. Replace the event loop entirely

Answer: B

Explanation: Microtasks allow quick, immediate async tasks.

19.   **Which queue is processed more frequently?**

A. Microtask queue is processed after every round of the event loop

B. Macrotask queue runs only once

C. They run at the same frequency

D. Macrotask queue runs before microtasks

Answer: A

Explanation: Microtasks are processed after each call stack clearing.

In which order will these logs appear?

```
console.log("A");
setTimeout(() => console.log("C"),0);
Promise.resolve().then(() => console.log("B"));
```

20.   A. A, B, C

B. A, C, B

C. B, A, C

D. C, B, A

Answer: A

Explanation: "A" (sync), then microtask "B", then macrotask "C".

10 Coding Exercises with Solutions and Explanations

Exercise 1: Promise vs SetTimeout Order

Task: Write code that uses `setTimeout()` and a `Promise.then()` and print the order of execution.

Solution:

```
console.log("Start");
setTimeout(() => console.log("Timeout"),0);
Promise.resolve().then(() =>
console.log("Microtask"));
```

```
console.log("End");
```

```
// Output:
```

```
// Start
```

```
// End
```

```
// Microtask
```

```
// Timeout
```

Explanation: Microtask (promise) runs before macrotask (timeout).

Exercise 2: Multiple Promises

Task: Queue multiple `.then()` calls and show they run in order before setTimeout.

Solution:

```
console.log("A");
Promise.resolve()
    .then(() => console.log("B"))
    .then(() => console.log("C"));
setTimeout(() => console.log("D"), 0);
// Output:
// A
// B
// C
// D
```

Explanation: All promise `.then()` handlers run before "D".

Exercise 3: queueMicrotask

Task: Use queueMicrotask() and setTimeout() and show
that queueMicrotask() runs first.

Solution:

```
console.log("1");
queueMicrotask(() => console.log("microtask"));
setTimeout(() => console.log("macrotask"), 0);
console.log("2");
// Output:
// 1
// 2
// microtask
// macrotask
```

Explanation: queueMicrotask executes before setTimeout.

Exercise 4: chain of microtasks

Task: Use a promise .then() that adds another .then() and
show all run before setTimeout.

Solution:

```
Promise.resolve("X")
  .then(res => {
    console.log(res);
    return "Y";
  })
  .then(res => console.log(res));
setTimeout(() => console.log("Z"), 0);
```

```
// Output:
```
```
// X
```
```
// Y
```
```
// Z
```
Explanation: Both `.then()` callbacks run before timeout "Z".

Exercise 5: MutationObserver (microtask)

Task: Use `MutationObserver` to trigger a callback and compare with setTimeout.

Solution:
```
let div = document.createElement('div');
document.body.appendChild(div);
const observer = new MutationObserver(() =>
console.log("Mutation Microtask"));
observer.observe(div, { childList: true });
setTimeout(() => console.log("Timeout
Macrotask"), 0);
div.appendChild(document.createTextNode('Hello'))
;
// Output:
// Mutation Microtask
// Timeout Macrotask
```
Explanation: MutationObserver callback is a microtask, runs before timeout.

(If running in Node, skip this exercise or simulate scenario.)

Exercise 6: Microtask in a microtask

Task: Add a .then() inside another .then() and show it still executes before a timeout.

Solution:

```
console.log("Start");
Promise.resolve()
   .then(() => {
      console.log("First then");
      Promise.resolve().then(() =>
console.log("Second then"));
   });
setTimeout(() => console.log("Timeout"),0);
// Output:
// Start
// First then
// Second then
// Timeout
```

Explanation: The second .then() is enqueued as a microtask and runs before the timeout.

Exercise 7: Ensuring microtasks run after synchronous code

Task: Use Promise.resolve().then() to ensure a log runs after a synchronous log.

Solution:

```
console.log("Synchronous log");
Promise.resolve().then(() =>
console.log("Microtask log"));
```

Explanation: The microtask runs after synchronous code finishes.

Exercise 8: Compare multiple setTimeouts and one promise

Task: Add multiple setTimeouts and one promise `.then()`, show the `.then()` executes before all timeouts.

Solution:

```
setTimeout(() => console.log("Timeout1"), 0);
setTimeout(() => console.log("Timeout2"), 0);
Promise.resolve().then(() =>
console.log("Microtask from promise"));
setTimeout(() => console.log("Timeout3"), 0);
// Output:
// Microtask from promise
// Timeout1
// Timeout2
// Timeout3
```

Explanation: Promise microtask runs first, then all timeouts in order.

Exercise 9: Using async/await to produce microtasks

Task: Use an async function and await `Promise.resolve()` to show microtask behavior.

Solution:

```
async function run() {
  console.log("Before await");
  await Promise.resolve();
  console.log("After await");
}
```

```
run();
console.log("End");
// Output:
// Before await
// End
// After await
```

Explanation: `await` resolved promise yields, placing "After await" in the microtask queue after the synchronous "End" finishes.

Exercise 10: Order of operations with nested calls

Task: Combine setTimeout, Promise, and queueMicrotask to show final order.

Solution:

```
console.log("A");
setTimeout(() => console.log("Macrotask"), 0);
Promise.resolve().then(() => {
  console.log("Promise1");
  queueMicrotask(() => console.log("Microtask
from queueMicrotask"));
});
Promise.resolve().then(() =>
console.log("Promise2"));
console.log("B");
// Output:
// A
// B
```

```
// Promise1
// Microtask from queueMicrotask
// Promise2
// Macrotask
```

Explanation: The order is: synchronous logs "A","B" → promise1

→ queueMicrotask → promise2 → finally macrotask from

setTimeout.

Summary

- **Microtasks:** Small callbacks that run immediately after the current synchronous code finishes, before any new macrotask. Examples: Promise `.then()`, `queueMicrotask()`.
- **Tasks (Macrotasks):** Larger asynchronous operations scheduled by `setTimeout`, `setInterval`, or I/O events run after all microtasks are done.

This distinction ensures promises and other microtasks have a higher priority, allowing more predictable async flow without waiting for the next macrotask cycle.

By practicing with the provided examples, questions, and exercises, you should now have a clear understanding of the differences and interplay between the task queue and microtask queue in the JavaScript event loop.

Understanding Multiple Promise Handling Methods

When working with asynchronous operations, you often deal with multiple promises. JavaScript provides methods on the `Promise` object to handle multiple promises at once:

1.   **`Promise.all(iterable)`**

   o   Takes an array (or iterable) of promises.

   o   Returns a single promise that fulfills when *all* of the input promises fulfill, or rejects if any one of them rejects.

   o   The result is an array of resolved values in the same order as the input promises.

2.   **`Promise.allSettled(iterable)`**

   o   Takes an array of promises.

   o   Returns a promise that resolves once *all* promises have settled (either fulfilled or rejected).

   o   The result is an array of objects, each describing the outcome (`status: "fulfilled"` or `"rejected"`) and the value or reason.

3.   **`Promise.race(iterable)`**

   o   Takes multiple promises.

   o   Returns a promise that resolves or rejects as soon as the first promise in the iterable settles.

   o   The result is the value of the first settled promise, no matter if it fulfilled or rejected.

4.   **`Promise.any(iterable)`**

- Takes multiple promises.
- Returns a promise that fulfills as soon as the first promise fulfills.
- If all promises reject, it rejects with an `AggregateError`.

When to Use Which?

- **`Promise.all`:**
Use when you want all results, or you need to fail if any one fails.
- **`Promise.allSettled`:**
Use when you want to wait for everything to finish regardless of success or failure, and then handle results accordingly.
- **`Promise.race`:**
Use when you want the first result, whether success or failure. Useful for timeouts or fastest response scenarios.
- **`Promise.any`:**
Use when you only need the first successful fulfillment and you don't care about failures (except if they all fail).

Code Examples

`Promise.all` Example:

```
const p1 = Promise.resolve(1);
const p2 = Promise.resolve(2);
const p3 = Promise.resolve(3);
Promise.all([p1, p2, p3])
    .then(results => {
```

```
    console.log(results); // [1,2,3]
  })
  .catch(error => console.error(error));
```

Promise.allSettled Example:

```
const p4 = Promise.resolve('ok');
const p5 = Promise.reject('error');
Promise.allSettled([p4, p5])
  .then(results => {
    console.log(results);
    // [
    //   {status: "fulfilled", value: "ok"},
    //   {status: "rejected", reason: "error"}
    // ]
  });
```

Promise.race Example:

```
const slow = new Promise(resolve => setTimeout(()
=> resolve('slow'), 1000));
const fast = new Promise(resolve => setTimeout(()
=> resolve('fast'), 100));
Promise.race([slow, fast]).then(result =>
console.log(result)); // "fast"
```

Promise.any Example:

```
const pFail1 = Promise.reject("fail1");
const pFail2 = Promise.reject("fail2");
const pSuccess = Promise.resolve("success");
```

```
Promise.any([pFail1, pFail2, pSuccess])
  .then(value => console.log(value)) // "success"
  .catch(error => console.error(error));
```

Multiple-Choice Questions

1.   **What does `Promise.all()` do?**

A. Returns a promise that fulfills only when all given promises fulfill.

B. Returns a promise that resolves if any promise resolves.

C. Returns when the first promise resolves or rejects.

D. Returns after all promises settle, no matter what.

Answer: A

Explanation: `Promise.all` waits for all to fulfill or one to reject.

2.   **What happens if any promise in `Promise.all([ ...` `])` rejects?**

A. The final promise never settles.

B. The final promise rejects immediately with that reason.

C. The final promise fulfills with an empty array.

D. The final promise waits for others anyway.

Answer: B

Explanation: `Promise.all` rejects as soon as one promise rejects.

3.   **If you want to get results of all promises regardless of rejection, which do you use?**

A. Promise.all

B. Promise.allSettled

C. Promise.race

D. Promise.any

Answer: B

Explanation: `allSettled` gives you the outcome of all promises (fulfilled or rejected).

4. **Which returns an array of objects with `status` and value/reason?**

A. Promise.all

B. Promise.allSettled

C. Promise.race

D. Promise.any

Answer: B

Explanation: `allSettled` returns detailed results for each promise.

5. **Which method returns as soon as the first promise settles (fulfills or rejects)?**

A. Promise.all

B. Promise.allSettled

C. Promise.race

D. Promise.any

Answer: C

Explanation: `Promise.race` settles with the first settled promise.

6. **If `Promise.race([p1, p2])` where p1 fulfills in 500ms and p2 rejects in 100ms, what happens?**

A. The final promise rejects after 100ms.

B. The final promise fulfills after 500ms.

C. It waits for all.

D. It never settles.

Answer: A

Explanation: The first settled is p2 rejecting at 100ms, so race rejects first.

7. **Which method returns the value of the first fulfilled promise and ignores rejections unless all fail?**

A. Promise.all

B. Promise.allSettled

C. Promise.race

D. Promise.any

Answer: D

Explanation: `Promise.any` returns first fulfilled promise, rejects only if all reject.

8. **What error is thrown if `Promise.any` fails all promises?**

A. TypeError

B. AggregateError

C. ReferenceError

D. SyntaxError

Answer: B

Explanation: `Promise.any` rejects with an `AggregateError`.

9. **If `Promise.all([])` is called with an empty array, what happens?**

A. Rejects immediately

B. Fulfills immediately with an empty array

C. Hangs forever

D. Throws an error

Answer: B

Explanation: With no promises, it resolves immediately with [ ].

10. **If Promise.allSettled is given all rejecting promises, what is the result?**

A. A promise that rejects

B. A promise that fulfills with an array of rejected statuses

C. A promise that never settles

D. A promise that returns the first rejected reason

Answer: B

Explanation: allSettled always fulfills, showing each promise's status (rejected or fulfilled).

11. **What does Promise.any return if one promise fulfills?**

A. The first fulfilled value

B. An array of all values

C. A rejection

D. Nothing

Answer: A

Explanation: any returns first successful fulfillment value.

12. **Which method can help create a timeout mechanism by racing a fetch call against a delay promise?**

A. Promise.all

B. Promise.allSettled

C. Promise.race

D. Promise.any

Answer: C

Explanation: race is ideal for timeouts—whichever settles first wins.

13.   **Promise.all short-circuits on:** A. first fulfillment

B. first rejection

C. never short-circuits

D. completion of all

Answer: B

Explanation: If any promise rejects, all stops and rejects immediately.

14.   **What happens if Promise.any receives only rejected promises?**

A. It rejects with an AggregateError after all rejections.

B. It rejects on the first rejection.

C. It fulfills with undefined.

D. It never settles.

Answer: A

Explanation: If none fulfill, it rejects with AggregateError.

15.   **If using Promise.all with a mix of resolved and rejected promises, what's the outcome?**

A. Rejects with the first rejection reason.

B. Fulfills with partial results.

C. Fulfills ignoring rejects.

D. All never settles.

Answer: A

Explanation: Promise.all rejects if any promise rejects.

16.   **In Promise.allSettled, if all promises are fulfilled, what's returned?**

A. A rejected promise.

B. A fulfilled promise with statuses all 'fulfilled'.

C. An error.

D. It's identical to Promise.all in that case.

Answer: B

Explanation: allSettled returns an array of objects with `status:"fulfilled"`.

17. **Which method ensures you always get results of all promises, even if some fail?**

A. Promise.all

B. Promise.allSettled

C. Promise.race

D. Promise.any

Answer: B

Explanation: `allSettled` gives outcomes for all regardless of success/failure.

18. **Is the order of results from `Promise.all` the same as the order of the input promises?**

A. Yes, order is preserved.

B. No, order is arbitrary.

C. It depends on which promise resolves first.

D. Results are sorted alphabetically.

Answer: A

Explanation: `Promise.all` results correspond to input order, not resolution order.

19. **If `Promise.race` gets one promise fulfilling after 1s and another rejecting after 500ms, what happens?**

A. Fulfills at 1s

B. Rejects at 500ms

C. Waits for both

D. Results in an empty array

Answer: B

Explanation: The rejected one settles first (500ms), so race rejects at that time.

20.   **If you need the first success no matter how many fail first, use:**

A. Promise.all

B. Promise.allSettled

C. Promise.race

D. Promise.any

Answer: D

Explanation: any returns the first successfully fulfilled promise.

10 Coding Exercises with Full Solutions and Explanations

Exercise 1: Using Promise.all

Task: Create two promises: one resolves with "A" after 100ms, another with "B" after 200ms. Use Promise.all to log both results.

Solution:

```
function delay(value, ms) {
  return new Promise(resolve => setTimeout(() =>
resolve(value), ms));
}

Promise.all([delay("A", 100), delay("B", 200)])
```

```
  .then(results => console.log(results)) // ["A",
"B"] after ~200ms
  .catch(error => console.error(error));
```
Explanation: Waits for both promises; logs ["A","B"] when both complete.

Exercise 2: Promise.all Rejection

Task: One promise rejects, another resolves. Show that `Promise.all` rejects.

Solution:
```
const p1 = Promise.resolve("Success");
const p2 = Promise.reject("Error occurred");
Promise.all([p1, p2])
  .then(values => console.log(values))
  .catch(err => console.log("Caught:", err)); //
"Caught: Error occurred"
```
Explanation: p2 rejects, so Promise.all rejects immediately.

Exercise 3: Using Promise.allSettled

Task: Combine one resolved and one rejected promise with `Promise.allSettled`.

Solution:
```
const p1 = Promise.resolve("OK");
const p2 = Promise.reject("Fail");
Promise.allSettled([p1, p2])
  .then(results => console.log(results));
// [
//   { status: "fulfilled", value: "OK" },
```

```
//    { status: "rejected", reason: "Fail" }
// ]
```
Explanation: allSettled returns both outcomes.

Exercise 4: Promise.race example

Task: Race two promises: one resolves in 500ms, another in 300ms, log which finishes first.

Solution:

```
const fast = new Promise(resolve => setTimeout(()
=> resolve("fast"), 300));
const slow = new Promise(resolve => setTimeout(()
=> resolve("slow"), 500));
Promise.race([fast, slow])
    .then(value => console.log(value)); // "fast"
```

Explanation: The promise that resolves first ("fast") wins the race.

Exercise 5: Promise.race with rejection

Task: Race a resolve promise at 1s and a reject promise at 500ms, see what happens.

Solution:

```
const rejectQuick = new Promise((_, reject) =>
setTimeout(() => reject("error"), 500));
const resolveSlow = new Promise(resolve =>
setTimeout(() => resolve("done"), 1000));
Promise.race([rejectQuick, resolveSlow])
    .then(value => console.log("Fulfilled:",
value))
    .catch(err => console.log("Rejected:", err));
```

```
// "Rejected: error" after 500ms
```

Explanation: The first to settle is rejectQuick (500ms), so race rejects.

Exercise 6: Promise.any success

Task: Use `Promise.any` with one failing promise and one successful promise.

Solution:

```
const fail = Promise.reject("nope");
const success = Promise.resolve("yay");
Promise.any([fail, success])
   .then(value => console.log("First success:",
value)) // "First success: yay"
   .catch(err => console.log("All failed:", err));
```

Explanation: any returns first successful result "yay".

Exercise 7: Promise.any all fail

Task: `Promise.any` with all rejecting promises; handle the AggregateError.

Solution:

```
const p1 = Promise.reject("err1");
const p2 = Promise.reject("err2");
Promise.any([p1, p2])
  .then(value => console.log(value))
  .catch(err => {
    console.log("All failed:", err.errors); //
["err1", "err2"]
  });
```

Explanation: If all fail, any rejects with AggregateError containing all errors.

Exercise 8: Using Promise.all for parallel fetches

Task: Fetch data from two URLs in parallel with `Promise.all` and display combined results.

Solution: *(Assuming environment supports fetch)*

```
Promise.all([

  fetch("https://jsonplaceholder.typicode.com/todos
/1").then(r => r.json()),

  fetch("https://jsonplaceholder.typicode.com/todos
/2").then(r => r.json())
])
.then(results => {
  console.log("Data:", results);
})
.catch(err => console.error("Error:", err));
```

Explanation: Both fetches run in parallel, results returned once both complete.

Exercise 9: Using Promise.any for fallback

Task: You have multiple endpoints. Use `Promise.any` to get data from whichever endpoint is fastest/successful.

Solution:

```
const endpoint1 =
fetch("https://example.com/fast").then(r =>
r.json());
const endpoint2 =
fetch("https://example.com/slow").then(r =>
r.json());
const endpoint3 = Promise.reject("Not
available");
Promise.any([endpoint1, endpoint2, endpoint3])
   .then(result => console.log("Got data from
fastest endpoint:", result))
   .catch(err => console.error("All failed:",
err));
```

Explanation: any returns the first successful response.

Exercise 10: Timeout a Promise with Promise.race

Task: Implement a timeout mechanism using Promise.race. If fetch takes too long, reject with a timeout error.

Solution:

```
function timeout(ms) {
   return new Promise((_, reject) => setTimeout(()
=> reject(new Error("Timeout")), ms));
}
Promise.race([
```

```
fetch("https://jsonplaceholder.typicode.com/todos
/1").then(r => r.json()),
   timeout(500) // If fetch not done in 500ms,
reject
])
.then(data => console.log("Fetch succeeded:",
data))
.catch(err => console.error("Error:", err));
```
Explanation: If fetch is slow, timeout promise rejects first, causing race to reject.

Summary

- **Promise.all**: Waits for all promises to fulfill or rejects immediately if one fails.
- **Promise.allSettled**: Waits for all promises to settle, returns detailed outcomes.
- **Promise.race**: Resolves or rejects as soon as the first promise settles.
- **Promise.any**: Resolves as soon as one promise fulfills, rejects only if all reject.

Understanding these methods allows handling multiple async operations elegantly, choosing the right tool depending on whether you need all results, partial results, or just the quickest or first successful result.

Introduction to Event-Driven Programming in JavaScript

Event-driven programming is a paradigm in which the flow of the program is determined by events—user actions like clicks, keyboard presses, and mouse movements; system-generated events like network responses; or developer-defined custom events. JavaScript's event-driven model is especially prominent in the browser environment, where the user interface (UI) continuously responds to user interactions and other triggers.

Key points:

- **Events** are signals that something has occurred.
- **Event Listeners (Handlers)** are functions that are called in response to a particular event.
- **DOM Events** target elements within a web page. For example, a button is clicked, an input field changes, or a form is submitted.
- **Custom Events** can be created and dispatched by developers to signal specific actions or state changes in their applications.

The Event Flow

When an event occurs on a specific DOM element, it doesn't just affect that element. Events propagate through the DOM in three phases:

1. **Capture phase**: The event travels down the DOM tree from the document root to the target element.

2. **Target phase**: The event reaches the target element where it actually originated.

3. **Bubble phase**: The event then bubbles up from the target element back up to the document root.

By default, event handlers listen in the bubble phase unless specified otherwise.

Adding and Removing Event Listeners

The primary method to register event listeners is
`addEventListener()`:

```
const button =
document.getElementById('myButton');
function handleClick(event) {
  console.log('Button was clicked!', event);
}
button.addEventListener('click', handleClick);
```

To remove the listener later:

```
button.removeEventListener('click', handleClick);
```

Common Event Types:

- **Mouse Events**: `click`, `dblclick`, `mousedown`, `mouseup`, `mouseenter`, `mouseleave`, `mouseover`, `mouseout`.

- **Keyboard Events**: `keydown`, `keyup`, `keypress`.

- **Form Events**: `submit`, `change`, `input`, `focus`, `blur`.

- **Window Events**: `load`, `resize`, `scroll`, `unload`.

Event Object

Every event listener receives an event object that provides information about the event:

- `event.target`: The element that triggered the event.
- `event.currentTarget`: The element the event listener is bound to.
- `event.type`: The type of the event (e.g., 'click').
- Mouse events have `pageX`, `pageY`, `clientX`, `clientY`.
- Keyboard events have `key`, `code`.

Example:

```
document.addEventListener('click',
function(event) {
  console.log('Clicked element:', event.target);
  console.log('Event type:', event.type);
});
```

Event Propagation and stopPropagation()

By default, events bubble up. You can control propagation with:

- `event.stopPropagation()` to prevent further bubbling.
- `event.stopImmediatePropagation()` to stop any further listeners on the same element as well.

- event.preventDefault() to prevent default browser actions (e.g., prevent a form from submitting).

Example:

```
document.getElementById('child').addEventListener
('click', function(event) {
  console.log('Child clicked');
  event.stopPropagation();
});
document.getElementById('parent').addEventListene
r('click', function() {
  console.log('Parent clicked');
});
```

If the user clicks the child element, normally "Parent clicked" would also log. With stopPropagation(), it stops at the child.

Using Capture Phase

To listen during the capture phase, pass true as the third argument to addEventListener():

```
document.getElementById('parent').addEventListene
r('click', function() {
  console.log('Parent capturing');
}, true);
```

Custom Events

You can create and dispatch your own events using the CustomEvent constructor and dispatchEvent():

```
const myElement =
document.getElementById('myElement');
myElement.addEventListener('myCustomEvent',
function(event) {
  console.log('Received my custom event:',
event.detail);
});
const customEvent = new
CustomEvent('myCustomEvent', {
  detail: { message: 'Hello from custom event!' }
});
myElement.dispatchEvent(customEvent);
```

Explanation:

- detail can hold any data you want to pass with the custom event.

- myElement will receive myCustomEvent, triggering the listener and logging event.detail.

Multiple-Choice Questions with Answers and Explanations

1.   **Which method is used to attach an event listener to an element?**

A. `element.onEvent()`

B. `element.addEventListener()`

C. `element.attach()`

D. `element.setEvent()`

Answer: B. The standard method is `addEventListener()`.

2.   **Which of the following stops the event from continuing to bubble up the DOM?**

A. `event.preventDefault()`

B. `event.stopPropagation()`

C. `event.stopBubbling()`

D. `event.halt()`

Answer: B. `stopPropagation()` prevents further propagation of the event.

3.   **What is the correct order of event propagation phases?**

A. Bubbling -> Target -> Capturing

B. Target -> Capturing -> Bubbling

C. Capturing -> Target -> Bubbling

D. Capturing -> Bubbling -> Target

Answer: C. Events flow: Capturing -> Target -> Bubbling.

4.   **What property of the event object references the element that actually triggered the event?**

A. `event.currentTarget`

B. `event.trigger`

C. `event.target`

D. `event.source`

Answer: C. `event.target` is the element that originated the event.

5.   **To prevent a link from navigating to a new page when clicked, which method would you use?**

A. `event.stopPropagation()`

B. `event.preventDefault()`

C. `event.stopImmediatePropagation()`

D. `event.cancel()`

Answer: B. `preventDefault()` prevents the browser's default behavior (navigation in case of links).

6.   **What argument would you pass to `addEventListener()` to listen in the capture phase?**

A. `true` as the third argument

B. `false` as the second argument

C. `{capture: true}` as the third argument

D. Both A and C are correct ways

Answer: D. Older syntax uses a boolean `true`, newer syntax supports `{capture: true}`.

7.   **Which event fires when a user clicks on an element?**

A. `submit`

B. `change`

C. `click`

D. `keyup`

Answer: C. A `click` event is fired on mouse click.

8.   **What is the default event propagation phase if not specified?**

A. Capturing

B. Bubbling

C. Target phase only

D. None of the above

Answer: B. By default, event listeners are registered in the bubbling phase.

9.　**If you attach multiple event listeners of the same type on the same element, in what order are they triggered by default?**

A. The last attached fires first.

B. The first attached fires first.

C. They fire simultaneously.

D. The order is random.

Answer: B. Event listeners are invoked in the order they were registered.

10.　**Which method is used to remove an event listener?**

A. `element.removeEventListener()`

B. `element.detachListener()`

C. `element.unbind()`

D. `element.remove()`

Answer: A. `removeEventListener()` removes an event listener.

11.　**What does `event.currentTarget` refer to?**

A. The element that originated the event

B. The element on which the event listener is currently invoked

C. The window object

D. The document body

Answer: B. `event.currentTarget` is the element to which the event handler is attached.

12.   **To create a custom event, which constructor would you use?**

A. `new Event()` or `new CustomEvent()`

B. `new CreateEvent()`

C. `new MyEvent()`

D. `document.createEvent()` (old API)

Answer: A. `Event` or `CustomEvent` constructors are used. `CustomEvent` allows `detail`.

13.   **What does the `detail` property in a CustomEvent represent?**

A. The type of event

B. A read-only timestamp

C. Arbitrary data passed when the event was created

D. The default action of the event

Answer: C. `detail` holds arbitrary custom data.

14.   **Which event is fired when a form is submitted?**

A. `click`

B. `submit`

C. `change`

D. `load`

Answer: B. `submit` fires when a form is submitted.

15.   **How do you listen to a key press event on a text input?**

A. `input.addEventListener('keypress', handler)`

B. `input.addEventListener('keydown', handler)`

C. `input.addEventListener('keyup', handler)`

D. All of the above (depending on desired event)

Answer: D. Key-related events can be `keydown`, `keyup`, or `keypress`. Which one you choose depends on the scenario.

16.   **What method do you call to trigger a custom event programmatically?**

A. `element.fire()`

B. `element.callEvent()`

C. `element.dispatchEvent()`

D. `element.emit()`

Answer: C. `dispatchEvent()` is used to trigger (dispatch) an event.

17.   **If `stopImmediatePropagation()` is called inside an event llstener, what happens?**

A. It stops other listeners on the same element from being called.

B. It stops event propagation up the DOM.

C. It prevents default browser action.

D. It does nothing different from `stopPropagation()`.

Answer: A. `stopImmediatePropagation()` prevents other event listeners on the same element from firing.

18.   **Which of the following can be listened to using `addEventListener()`?**

A. DOM elements

B. The window object

C. Document object

D. All of the above

Answer: D. All of these implement EventTarget, so you can add event listeners.

19. **If you have multiple nested elements and the user clicks the inner one, where does the event first arrive during capturing?**

A. The target element

B. The document

C. The window

D. The deepest nested element first

Answer: B. Capturing starts from the top (document) down to the target.

20. **Which mouse event is fired when the mouse pointer moves onto an element?**

A. `mouseover`

B. `mouseout`

C. `mouseenter`

D. `click`

Answer: A. `mouseover` is fired when the pointer enters the element's area. (Note: `mouseenter` is similar but doesn't bubble.)

10 Coding Exercises with Solutions and Explanations

1. Click Event on a Button

Exercise: Add a "click" event listener to a button with id="myBtn" that logs "Button clicked!".

Solution:

```html
<button id="myBtn">Click me</button>
<script>
  const btn = document.getElementById('myBtn');
  btn.addEventListener('click', function() {
    console.log('Button clicked!');
  });
</script>
```

Explanation: When the user clicks the button, the event listener logs the message.

2. Prevent Default Link Behavior

Exercise: Given a link `<a href="http://example.com" id="myLink">Go to Example</a>`, prevent navigation when clicked and instead log "Link clicked but no navigation".

Solution:

```html
<a href="http://example.com" id="myLink">Go to Example</a>
<script>
  const link = document.getElementById('myLink');
  link.addEventListener('click', function(event) {
    event.preventDefault();
    console.log('Link clicked but no navigation');
```

```
    });
</script>
```

Explanation: Using `preventDefault()` stops the link from navigating.

3. Stopping Event Propagation

Exercise: Suppose we have:

```
<div id="parent">
  <div id="child">Click me</div>
</div>
```

Attach a click listener to both #parent and #child. Make the child's event stop propagation so only "Child clicked" is logged, not "Parent clicked".

Solution:

```
<div id="parent">
  <div id="child">Click me</div>
</div>
<script>

document.getElementById('child').addEventListener
('click', function(event) {
    console.log('Child clicked');
    event.stopPropagation();
  });
```

```
document.getElementById('parent').addEventListene
r('click', function() {
    console.log('Parent clicked');
  });
</script>
```

Explanation: `stopPropagation()` prevents the parent's event handler from firing.

4. Listening in Capture Phase

Exercise: Using the same `parent` and `child` elements, add a listener to the parent that fires during capture phase. Log "Parent capturing".

Solution:

```
<div id="parent">
  <div id="child">Click me</div>
</div>
<script>

document.getElementById('parent').addEventListene
r('click', function() {
    console.log('Parent capturing');
  }, true);
```

```
document.getElementById('child').addEventListener
('click', function() {
    console.log('Child clicked');
  });
</script>
```

Explanation: Passing `true` makes the parent's event run on capture before reaching the child.

5. Key Press Event

Exercise: Listen for the `keydown` event on `document` and log the pressed key.
Solution:

```
<script>
  document.addEventListener('keydown',
function(event) {
    console.log('Key pressed:', event.key);
  });
</script>
```

Explanation: `event.key` gives the character of the pressed key.

6. Removing an Event Listener

Exercise: Attach a click event listener to a button that logs "Clicked". After the first click, remove the event listener, so subsequent clicks do nothing.

Solution:

```html
<button id="onceBtn">Click once</button>
<script>
  const btn = document.getElementById('onceBtn');
  function handleClick() {
    console.log('Clicked');
    btn.removeEventListener('click',
handleClick);
  }
  btn.addEventListener('click', handleClick);
</script>
```

Explanation: On the first click, we run `removeEventListener()` to remove the handler.

7. Custom Event Dispatch

Exercise: Create a custom event called "myEvent" and dispatch it on a div with id="myDiv". The event should log "Custom event received!" when handled.

Solution:

```html
<div id="myDiv"></div>
<script>
  const div = document.getElementById('myDiv');
  div.addEventListener('myEvent', function() {
    console.log('Custom event received!');
  });
```

```
const customEvent = new CustomEvent('myEvent');
div.dispatchEvent(customEvent);
</script>
```

Explanation: We create a `CustomEvent` and `dispatchEvent()` on the element that listens for it.

8. Using event.detail in CustomEvent

Exercise: Dispatch a custom event named "showMessage" with a detail `{text: 'Hello World'}` and log the detail in the event handler.

Solution:

```
<div id="messageBox"></div>
<script>
  const box =
document.getElementById('messageBox');
  box.addEventListener('showMessage',
function(event) {
    console.log('Message:', event.detail.text);
  });
  const showMessageEvent = new
CustomEvent('showMessage', {
    detail: { text: 'Hello World' }
  });
  box.dispatchEvent(showMessageEvent);
</script>
```

Explanation: `event.detail` provides the passed data.

9. Event Delegation

Exercise: Given a list of items:

```
<ul id="list">
  <li>Item 1</li>
  <li>Item 2</li>
</ul>
```

Use event delegation on `ul#list` to log which item was clicked without adding a listener to each `li`.

Solution:

```
<ul id="list">
  <li>Item 1</li>
  <li>Item 2</li>
</ul>
<script>
  const ul = document.getElementById('list');
  ul.addEventListener('click', function(event) {
    if (event.target.tagName === 'LI') {
      console.log('Clicked on:',
event.target.textContent);
    }
  });
</script>
```

Explanation: Using `event.target` we detect the clicked `li`. This is event delegation.

10. Preventing Default Submit

Exercise: Given a form:

```
<form id="myForm">
  <input type="text" name="name" />
  <button type="submit">Submit</button>
</form>
```

Prevent the default submit action and log the input's value.

Solution:

```
<form id="myForm">
  <input type="text" name="name" />
  <button type="submit">Submit</button>
</form>
<script>
  const form = document.getElementById('myForm');
  form.addEventListener('submit', function(event) {
    event.preventDefault();
    const nameValue = form.elements['name'].value;
    console.log('Form submitted with name:', nameValue);
  });
```

```
</script>
```

Explanation: `preventDefault()` stops the page refresh. We then access the form field value and log it.

Conclusion

Event-driven programming in JavaScript revolves around attaching listeners, handling events gracefully, managing propagation, and occasionally customizing or creating new events. Mastering these concepts is crucial for building interactive and responsive web applications. The provided examples, questions, and exercises help reinforce these principles and best practices.

Understanding JavaScript Web APIs

JavaScript by itself provides core language features, but in a browser environment, you have access to various Web APIs implemented by the browser. These APIs allow you to perform asynchronous tasks, schedule code execution, make network requests, and handle animations.

setTimeout and setInterval

`setTimeout(callback, delay)`:
- Schedules a callback to run after a certain amount of milliseconds (delay).
- Returns a timeout ID that can be cleared with `clearTimeout(id)`.

Example:

```
console.log("Before");
setTimeout(() => {
  console.log("Ran after 1 second");
}, 1000);
console.log("After");
```

Order: "Before", "After", then after 1 second "Ran after 1 second".

setInterval(callback, delay):

● Schedules a callback to run repeatedly every given delay in milliseconds.

● Returns an interval ID that can be cleared with clearInterval(id).

Example:

```
let count = 0;
const intervalId = setInterval(() => {
  count++;
  console.log("Interval count:", count);
  if (count === 5) clearInterval(intervalId);
}, 1000);
```

Prints "Interval count:" from 1 to 5 every second, then stops.

fetch API

fetch(url, options):

● A modern way to make network requests returning a Promise.

● Returns a Response object when resolved.

- Often used with `async`/`await` and `response.json()` to parse JSON responses.

Example:

```
fetch('https://jsonplaceholder.typicode.com/todos
/1')
  .then(response => response.json())
  .then(data => console.log(data))
  .catch(error => console.error(error));
```

Using `async`/`await`:

```
async function getData() {
  try {
    const response = await
fetch('https://jsonplaceholder.typicode.com/todos
/1');
    const data = await response.json();
    console.log(data);
  } catch(e) {
    console.error(e);
  }
}
getData();
```

requestAnimationFrame

`requestAnimationFrame(callback)`:
- Schedules a callback to run before the next repaint.

- Used for smooth animations as it syncs with the browser's refresh rate.
- Callback receives a timestamp as an argument.
- Cancel with `cancelAnimationFrame(id)`.

Example:

```
let start = null;
function animate(time) {
  if (!start) start = time;
  const elapsed = time - start;
  // Move a box 100px in 1 second
  const x = Math.min(100 * (elapsed / 1000), 100);
  document.getElementById('box').style.transform = `translateX(${x}px)`;
  if (x < 100) {
    requestAnimationFrame(animate);
  }
}
requestAnimationFrame(animate);
```

Multiple-Choice Questions

1. **What does `setTimeout` do?**
A. Runs a function immediately
B. Schedules a function to run after a specified delay
C. Repeats a function at regular intervals

D. Fetches data from a server

Answer: B

Explanation: setTimeout schedules code to run once after a certain time.

2.   **What is returned by `setInterval`?**

A. A promise

B. An interval ID that can be used with `clearInterval`

C. A response object

D. Nothing

Answer: B

Explanation: setInterval returns an ID for clearing the interval.

3.   **If you want to stop a `setTimeout` callback from running, what do you call?**

A. `clearInterval()`

B. `cancelAnimationFrame()`

C. `clearTimeout()`

D. `stopTimeout()`

Answer: C

Explanation: `clearTimeout` stops a scheduled timeout.

4.   **Which Web API is used to make network requests that returns a promise?**

A. fetch

B. setInterval

C. requestAnimationFrame

D. JSON.parse

Answer: A

Explanation: `fetch` is the modern API for network requests returning a promise.

5. **Which method would you use for smooth animations synchronized with the browser's repaint?**

A. setTimeout

B. setInterval

C. requestAnimationFrame

D. fetch

Answer: C

Explanation: requestAnimationFrame is designed for smooth, efficient animations.

6. **What does the then method on fetch's returned promise provide?**

A. Immediate value

B. Callback for when the fetch resolves

C. A way to convert to JSON automatically

D. It doesn't exist

Answer: B

Explanation: then attaches callbacks for when a promise (like from fetch) resolves.

7. **How do you parse JSON from a fetch response?**

A. `response.text()`

B. `response.json()`

C. `JSON.parse(response)` directly

D. `response.jsonparse()`

Answer: B

Explanation: `response.json()` returns a promise that resolves to parsed JSON.

8.   **If `setInterval` is set to 1000ms, how often does the callback run?**

A. Once after 1s

B. Every 1 second, repeatedly

C. Every time user clicks

D. Never

Answer: B

Explanation: setInterval repeats the callback every specified delay.

9.   **How to cancel an animation frame requested by requestAnimationFrame?**

A. `clearTimeout()`

B. `clearInterval()`

C. `cancelAnimationFrame()`

D. `stopAnimation()`

Answer: C

Explanation: `cancelAnimationFrame(id)` cancels a requested animation frame.

10.   **If `setTimeout` is given a delay of 0, when does the callback run?**

A. Immediately, before any other code

B. After currently executing code and all microtasks, as soon as possible

C. Never

D. At exactly 0ms

Answer: B

Explanation: setTimeout 0ms runs after the current call stack clears and microtasks complete.

11.   **Which fetch call format is correct?**

A. `fetch("url").then(res => res.json())`

B. `fetch.then("url")`

C. `fetch("url", res => {...})`

D. `new fetch("url")`

Answer: A

Explanation: `fetch("url").then(...)` is the correct usage.

12.   **requestAnimationFrame callback receives what argument?**

A. The element being animated

B. A timestamp representing the current time

C. The number of frames per second

D. No arguments

Answer: B

Explanation: The callback gets a timestamp.

13.   **Which method schedules a single future execution of a function?**

A. setTimeout

B. setInterval

C. requestAnimationFrame

D. fetch

Answer: A

Explanation: setTimeout runs the callback once after a delay.

14.   **If a request fails when using fetch, how do you handle it?**

A. `then` always catches errors automatically

B. Use `.catch(...)` to handle errors

C. It's impossible to handle errors

D. Use setTimeout to retry

Answer: B

Explanation: Errors from fetch promises are handled using `catch`.

15.   **What is the recommended way to run code at the browser's refresh rate?**

A. setInterval(16)

B. requestAnimationFrame

C. setTimeout(0)

D. fetch

Answer: B

Explanation: requestAnimationFrame is designed for animations at the browser's refresh rate.

16.   **When does a setInterval callback stop running?**

A. Never, unless cleared with clearInterval()

B. After one call

C. When the page closes

D. It chooses randomly

Answer: A

Explanation: setInterval runs indefinitely until `clearInterval` is called or page closed.

17.   **Which API allows you to get a promise-based response for HTTP requests by default?**

A. XMLHttpRequest (old callback-based)

B. fetch (promise-based)

C. setTimeout

D. requestAnimationFrame

Answer: B

Explanation: fetch is promise-based for HTTP requests.

18.   **What is not true about fetch?**

A. It returns a promise

B. It rejects only on network errors by default, not on HTTP error statuses

C. It can handle binary data with response.blob()

D. It can parse JSON automatically without calling `json()`

Answer: D

Explanation: You must call `response.json()` to parse JSON, not automatic.

19.   **requestAnimationFrame is called how many times per second typically?**

A. Exactly once per second

B. Once per browser repaint (~60fps)

C. 100 times per second

D. Once every 10 seconds

Answer: B

Explanation: Typically matches browser refresh (~60 times per second).

20.   **To handle large JSON from fetch efficiently, you might:**

A. Use `response.json()` which returns a promise for the whole JSON

B. Use setInterval

C. Use requestAnimationFrame

D. You cannot handle large JSON

Answer: A

Explanation: `response.json()` is used to parse JSON fully once loaded.

10 Coding Exercises with Solutions and Explanations

Exercise 1: Using setTimeout

Task: Print "Hello" after 2 seconds using `setTimeout`.

Solution:

```
setTimeout(() => {
  console.log("Hello");
}, 2000);
```

Explanation: Runs the callback after 2000ms.

Exercise 2: Cancel a setTimeout

Task: Schedule a message, but cancel it before it runs.

Solution:

```
const id = setTimeout(() => console.log("This
won't run"), 1000);
clearTimeout(id);
```

Explanation: The timeout is cleared, so no log appears.

Exercise 3: setInterval Counting

Task: Use setInterval to log a counter every second. Stop after 5 counts.

Solution:

```
let count = 0;
```

```
const intervalId = setInterval(() => {
  count++;
  console.log(count);
  if (count >= 5) {
    clearInterval(intervalId);
  }
}, 1000);
```

Explanation: Interval prints numbers 1 to 5 then stops.

Exercise 4: Simple fetch request

Task: Fetch JSON from a placeholder API and log the title property.

Solution:

```
fetch('https://jsonplaceholder.typicode.com/todos
/1')
  .then(response => response.json())
  .then(data => console.log(data.title));
```

Explanation: Fetches data and logs `data.title`.

Exercise 5: Handle fetch errors

Task: Try fetching an invalid URL and catch the error.

Solution:

```
fetch('https://invalid.url')
  .then(res => res.json())
  .then(data => console.log(data))
  .catch(err => console.error("Error:", err));
```

Explanation: `catch` handles network errors.

Exercise 6: requestAnimationFrame to animate a box

Task: Move a box from left to right using requestAnimationFrame.

Solution (assuming element with id='box'):

```
let start = null;
function animate(time) {
  if (!start) start = time;
  const elapsed = time - start;
  const x = Math.min(elapsed/10, 200); // move
right by elapsed/10 px, max 200px
  document.getElementById('box').style.transform
= `translateX(${x}px)`;
  if (x < 200) requestAnimationFrame(animate);
}
requestAnimationFrame(animate);
```

Explanation: Animates smoothly with requestAnimationFrame.

Exercise 7: Abort a requestAnimationFrame

Task: Start an animation and cancel it after 500ms.

Solution:

```
let startTime;
let animationId;
function move(time) {
  if (!startTime) startTime = time;
  const elapsed = time - startTime;
  document.getElementById('box').style.transform
= `translateX(${elapsed / 10}px)`;
  animationId = requestAnimationFrame(move);
```

```
}
// Start animation
animationId = requestAnimationFrame(move);
// Cancel after 500ms
setTimeout(() =>
cancelAnimationFrame(animationId), 500);
```

Explanation: Cancels the animation frame after half a second.

Exercise 8: Fetch multiple requests in sequence

Task: Fetch two URLs in sequence using fetch and await.

Solution (requires async/await):

```
async function fetchSequence() {
  const res1 = await
fetch('https://jsonplaceholder.typicode.com/todos
/1');
  const data1 = await res1.json();
  console.log('First:', data1.title);
  const res2 = await
fetch('https://jsonplaceholder.typicode.com/todos
/2');
  const data2 = await res2.json();
  console.log('Second:', data2.title);
}
fetchSequence();
```

Explanation: Runs one fetch after the previous completes.

Exercise 9: Using setInterval for a timer

Task: Display a countdown from 5 to 0 using setInterval, then log "Done".

Solution:

```
let timer = 5;
const tid = setInterval(() => {
  console.log(timer);
  timer--;
  if (timer < 0) {
    clearInterval(tid);
    console.log("Done");
  }
}, 1000);
```

Explanation: Every second decrement and log, then stop at 0 and say "Done".

Exercise 10: Animate using requestAnimationFrame for a fade-out effect

Task: Decrease the opacity of an element from 1 to 0 over 2 seconds.

Solution:

```
let startTime;
const element = document.getElementById('fade');
function fadeOut(timestamp) {
  if (!startTime) startTime = timestamp;
  const elapsed = timestamp - startTime;
  const duration = 2000; // 2 seconds
```

```
  const progress = Math.min(elapsed / duration,
1);
  element.style.opacity = 1 - progress;
  if (progress < 1) {
    requestAnimationFrame(fadeOut);
  }
}
requestAnimationFrame(fadeOut);
```
Explanation: Gradually reduces opacity, smooth animation.

Summary

- **setTimeout**: Schedules a single callback after a delay.
- **setInterval**: Repeats a callback at regular intervals.
- **fetch**: Makes network requests, returns promises.
- **requestAnimationFrame**: Schedules code before next repaint for smooth animations.

These Web APIs allow asynchronous code execution, network communication, timed callbacks, and browser-synced animations. Understanding these is crucial for building interactive and performant web applications.

Understanding Debouncing and Throttling in JavaScript

As web applications grow in complexity, performance optimizations become crucial. Two common techniques are **debouncing** and **throttling**. They help control how often a function is executed in response to events like scrolling, resizing, or typing, thereby improving performance and user experience.

Debouncing

What is Debouncing?

Debouncing ensures that a function is not called too frequently. Instead, it delays the function execution until a certain amount of "quiet" time has passed since the last call. If a user keeps triggering an event (like typing in a textbox), the debounced function only runs when the user stops triggering the event for a specified time.

How it Works:

- Every time the event fires, the debounce function clears the previous timer and sets a new one.
- If the event does not fire again within the specified delay, the function executes.
- If the event fires again before the delay, the timer resets, postponing execution.

Use Case:

- Handling input events (e.g., search input) where you only want to make an API request after the user stops typing.
- Window resize or scroll events, to avoid firing a callback on every pixel movement.

Example Debounce Implementation:

```
function debounce(func, delay) {
```

```
  let timeoutId;
  return function(...args) {
    clearTimeout(timeoutId);
    timeoutId = setTimeout(() => func.apply(this,
args), delay);
  };
}
// Usage:
const debouncedLogger = debounce(() =>
console.log("Debounced!"), 300);
window.addEventListener('scroll',
debouncedLogger);
```

This logs "Debounced!" only after the user stops scrolling for at least 300ms.

Throttling

What is Throttling?

Throttling ensures that a function runs at most once in a given time interval. If a user triggers events continuously, the throttled function executes immediately on the first event, and then only once per specified interval, ignoring calls that occur too frequently in between.

How it Works:

- When the event occurs, if the function hasn't been called in the last 'delay' ms, it runs immediately.

- Subsequent calls within the delay period are ignored until the delay time passes.

Use Case:

- Controlling the rate of firing scroll events for updating UI elements like a fixed header or infinite scroll logic.
- Handling window resize events only a certain number of times per second.

Example Throttle Implementation:

```
function throttle(func, delay) {
  let lastTime = 0;
  return function(...args) {
    const now = Date.now();
    if (now - lastTime >= delay) {
      func.apply(this, args);
      lastTime = now;
    }
  };
}
// Usage:
const throttledLogger = throttle(() =>
console.log("Throttled!"), 300);
window.addEventListener('scroll',
throttledLogger);
```

This logs "Throttled!" at most once every 300ms during scrolling.

Differences Between Debouncing and Throttling

- **Debounce:** Waits until a period of inactivity to call the function. Good for operations that should happen once the user has "finished" an action.
- **Throttle:** Guarantees the function runs at regular intervals, no matter how frequently the event is triggered.

Code Examples

Debounce Input:

```
const input = document.getElementById('search');
const debouncedSearch = debounce((query) => {
  console.log("Searching for:", query);
  // Imagine API call here
}, 500);
input.addEventListener('input', (e) => {
  debouncedSearch(e.target.value);
});
```

Throttle Scroll Handler:

```
const handleScroll = throttle(() => {
  console.log("Scroll handler called");
}, 200);
window.addEventListener('scroll', handleScroll);
```

Multiple-Choice Questions

1. **What does debouncing do?**

A. Executes a function repeatedly as fast as possible.

B. Ensures a function runs after it has not been called for a certain amount of time.

C. Limits function execution to at most once every interval.

D. Immediately runs the function on every event.

Answer: B

Explanation: Debouncing delays function execution until after a period of no calls.

2. **What does throttling do?**

A. Prevents a function from running at all.

B. Ensures a function runs at most once every given time interval.

C. Runs a function only after user input ends.

D. Speeds up function calls.

Answer: B

Explanation: Throttling limits frequency of function calls to a set interval.

3. **When is debounce most useful?**

A. When you need a function to run on every keystroke.

B. When you want a function to run only after the user stops an action for some time.

C. When you need regular periodic updates.

D. When you need immediate execution.

Answer: B

Explanation: Debounce is great for final actions after user finishes typing or interacting.

4. **When is throttle most useful?**

A. When immediate and frequent updates are fine.

B. When you only run a function once after activity stops.

C. When you need to ensure continuous event firing but at a controlled rate.

D. When you never want to skip calls.

Answer: C

Explanation: Throttle ensures periodic execution, good for controlling rate of execution.

5. **If you want a function to run once after no keypress has occurred for 500ms, you use:**

A. Throttle with 500ms

B. Debounce with 500ms

C. setInterval with 500ms

D. requestAnimationFrame

Answer: B

Explanation: Debounce waits for inactivity period.

6. **If you want a function to run at most once every 300ms while scrolling, use:**

A. Debounce(300ms)

B. Throttle(300ms)

C. No need, just call directly

D. setTimeout directly

Answer: B

Explanation: Throttling is ideal for limiting frequency during continuous events like scroll.

7. **Debounce vs Throttle difference:**

A. Debounce runs at regular intervals, throttle waits for inactivity.

B. Debounce waits until last event, throttle enforces a maximum call frequency.

C. Both are identical.

D. Throttle waits until last event, debounce at fixed intervals.

Answer: B

8.   **If a debounced function is called repeatedly every 100ms, and the delay is 300ms, when does it run?**

A. Immediately on first call

B. Every 100ms

C. After no calls occur for 300ms

D. Never

Answer: C

9.   **Throttled function with interval 200ms called continuously, it runs:**

A. Only once at end

B. Approximately every 200ms

C. Exactly every 1000ms

D. Never runs

Answer: B

10.   **Which approach helps prevent 'API calls on every keystroke' scenario?**

A. Throttling

B. Debouncing

C. Both

D. Neither

Answer: B

Explanation: Debouncing waits until typing stops.

11.   Which approach is best for updating scroll position indicators without overwhelming performance?

A. Debounce

B. Throttle

C. Neither

D. Both equally

Answer: B

Explanation: Throttle ensures periodic updates during continuous scrolling.

12.   Debounce is often used for:

A. Handling resize events after user stops resizing window

B. Ensuring constant updates every interval

C. Immediate execution on first event

D. Scheduling repeated tasks

Answer: A

13.   Throttle is often used for:

A. Running code only once after user input ends

B. Minimizing the number of times a function runs during continuous events

C. Delaying execution until a timeout

D. Parsing JSON quickly

Answer: B

14.   If you need immediate execution on first event and then restrict further calls, choose:

A. Debounce

B. Throttle

C. Both

D. None

Answer: B

Explanation: Throttle executes immediately and then waits before next call.

15.　　**In a throttle implementation, if event fires repeatedly, what happens to calls during 'cool-down' period?**

A. They accumulate and run after cool-down

B. They are ignored

C. They shorten the delay

D. They speed up calls

Answer: B

Explanation: Throttled calls during cooldown are ignored.

16.　　**In a debounce implementation, if event fires again before delay passes:**

A. The timer resets and function call is postponed

B. Function runs immediately

C. Timer shortens

D. Function never runs

Answer: A

17.　　**A good analogy for debouncing:**

A. A faucet dripping at fixed intervals (Throttle)

B. Waiting until user stops typing before searching (Debounce)

C. A stopwatch ticking constantly (Neither)

D. Immediate response to every input (No)

Answer: B

18.　　**A good analogy for throttling:**

A. Only allow a certain number of calls in a time window, like passing through a turnstile at intervals.

B. Wait for quiet period before action.

C. Run once at the end.

D. Never run.

Answer: A

19.   **Can you combine debouncing and throttling?**

A. No, they are incompatible

B. Yes, but it's uncommon. They solve different issues

C. Only in Node.js

D. Required always

Answer: B

Explanation: It's possible but they are usually used separately for different scenarios.

20.   **For a search input: user types quickly, you want to send AJAX request only after user stops typing:**

A. Use throttle

B. Use debounce

C. Use setInterval

D. Use no optimization

Answer: B

10 Coding Exercises with Full Solutions and Explanations

Exercise 1: Basic Debounce

Task: Create a debounce function. Log "Hello" only if no further calls happen for 500ms.

Solution:

```
function debounce(fn, delay) {
```

```
  let timer;
  return function(...args) {
    clearTimeout(timer);
    timer = setTimeout(() => fn.apply(this,
args), delay);
  };
}
const debouncedHello = debounce(() =>
console.log("Hello"), 500);
// If you call debouncedHello() multiple times
quickly, "Hello" only logs after user stops
calling for 0.5s.
debouncedHello();
debouncedHello();
// Wait and see only one "Hello" after 500ms
idle.
```

Explanation: The last call resets timer, so it waits until no calls occur for 500ms.

Exercise 2: Basic Throttle

Task: Create a throttle function that logs "Throttled!" at most once every 1000ms no matter how often called.

Solution:

```
function throttle(fn, delay) {
  let lastCall = 0;
```

```
  return function(...args) {
    const now = Date.now();
    if (now - lastCall >= delay) {
      lastCall = now;
      fn.apply(this, args);
    }
  };
}
const throttledLog = throttle(() =>
console.log("Throttled!"), 1000);
setInterval(throttledLog, 100); // Called every
100ms but logs only every 1000ms
```

Explanation: The throttle checks if enough time passed since last execution.

Exercise 3: Debounce Search Input

Task: On an input field's "input" event, use debounce to log the value after user stops typing for 300ms.

Solution:

```
const input = document.getElementById('search');
const debouncedHandler = debounce(value =>
console.log("Search:", value), 300);
input.addEventListener('input', e =>
debouncedHandler(e.target.value));
```

Explanation: The function logs the search term only after user stops typing for 300ms.

Exercise 4: Throttle Scroll Event

Task: Throttle a scroll event so a callback runs at most every 200ms.

Solution:

```
window.addEventListener('scroll', throttle(() =>
{
  console.log("Scrolled!");
}, 200));
```

Explanation: The console logs on scroll, but not on every pixel movement, only once every 200ms.

Exercise 5: Debounce Window Resize

Task: When window is resized, log the new window size after user stops resizing for 500ms.

Solution:

```
window.addEventListener('resize', debounce(() =>
{
  console.log(`Width: ${window.innerWidth},
Height: ${window.innerHeight}`);
}, 500));
```

Explanation: Only logs once resize stops for half a second.

Exercise 6: Immediate Throttle

Task: Modify throttle so that it also executes immediately on first call.

(The provided throttle already does so if enough time passed since lastCall=0. Just show code using it.)

Solution:

```
function immediateThrottle(fn, delay) {
  let lastCall = 0;
  return function(...args) {
    const now = Date.now();
    if (now - lastCall >= delay) {
      lastCall = now;
      fn.apply(this, args);
    }
  };
}
const logImmediate = immediateThrottle(() =>
console.log("Immediate throttle"), 1000);
window.addEventListener('scroll', logImmediate);
```

Explanation: The first scroll triggers immediately, then waits 1s for next run.

Exercise 7: Debounce with Leading Option

Task: Implement a debounce that also can run once immediately at the start (leading=true), then wait for inactivity.

Solution:

```
function debounce(fn, delay, leading = false) {
```

```
    let timer, invoked = false;
    return function(...args) {
      const callNow = leading && !invoked;
      clearTimeout(timer);
      timer = setTimeout(() => {
        timer = null;
        invoked = false;
        if (!leading) fn.apply(this, args);
      }, delay);
      if (callNow) {
        invoked = true;
        fn.apply(this, args);
      }
    };
}
const debouncedWithLeading = debounce(() =>
console.log("Run immediately and then wait"),
300, true);
debouncedWithLeading();
debouncedWithLeading();
// First call logs immediately, subsequent calls
reset timer.
```

Explanation: This advanced debounce runs once immediately if leading=true.

Exercise 8: Throttle a resizing event and show a counter

Task: Count how many times throttle callback fired during continuous resizing of the window every 200ms.

Solution:

```
let resizeCount = 0;
const throttledResize = throttle(() => {
  resizeCount++;
  console.log("Throttled resize count:",
resizeCount);
}, 200);
window.addEventListener('resize',
throttledResize);
```

Explanation: Only increments count at max once per 200ms, even if resize fires continuously.

Exercise 9: Debounce API call simulation

Task: Simulate an API call triggered by input, but only if user stops typing for 500ms.

Solution:

```
function simulateAPICall(query) {
  console.log("Fetching results for:", query);
}
const debouncedAPICall =
debounce(simulateAPICall, 500);
```

```
document.getElementById('search').addEventListene
r('input', e => {
  debouncedAPICall(e.target.value);
});
```

Explanation: The API simulation only runs when typing stops for half a second.

Exercise 10: Throttle a function in a loop

Task: Create a loop calling a throttled function every 50ms and see it run only every 300ms.

Solution:

```
const throttledFn = throttle(() =>
console.log("Called throttledFn"), 300);
let count = 0;
const intervalId = setInterval(() => {
  count++;
  if (count > 20) clearInterval(intervalId);
  throttledFn();
}, 50);
```

Explanation: Though called every 50ms, it prints "Called throttledFn" about every 300ms.

Summary

- **Debouncing**: Delays execution until a period of inactivity. Great for search boxes or window resize events, ensuring final action only after user stops interacting.
- **Throttling**: Limits execution to a maximum rate. Perfect for scroll events or other high-frequency actions, ensuring function runs at controlled intervals.

Mastering debouncing and throttling enhances performance and prevents unnecessary computations, improving overall user experience.

Introduction to the Fetch API

The Fetch API provides a modern, promise-based interface for making HTTP requests in JavaScript. Introduced as a more flexible and cleaner alternative to XMLHttpRequest (XHR), the Fetch API is natively available in modern browsers and can be used both in the browser environment and server-side (e.g., via Node.js if you include a polyfill like `node-fetch`).

Key characteristics of the Fetch API include:

- **Promise-based**: Instead of using callbacks or the XHR event model, `fetch()` returns a Promise, making it simpler to integrate with async/await and promise chains.
- **More modern and flexible**: Uses a Request and Response model which can be easily manipulated.
- **Streaming responses**: The body of a response can be accessed as a stream, allowing efficient handling of large data.

Basic Usage

The most basic usage of the Fetch API involves calling the `fetch()` function with a resource URL and then handling the returned promise. For example:

```
fetch('https://api.example.com/data')
  .then(response => {
    if (!response.ok) {
      throw new Error('Network response was not
ok ' + response.statusText);
    }
    return response.json(); // parse JSON body
  })
  .then(data => {
    console.log(data); // use the JSON data
  })
  .catch(error => {
    console.error('Fetch error:', error);
  });
```

Important Concepts:

1. **The `fetch()` function:**
   ○ Syntax: `fetch(input, [init])`
   ○ `input` can be a URL string or a `Request` object.

- init is an options object that can include method, headers, body, mode, credentials, etc.
2. **Response Handling**: The `fetch()` call returns a Response object, which has methods to read its body:
- `.text()` for plain text
- `.json()` for JSON data
- `.blob()`, `.arrayBuffer()`, `.formData()` for other data formats.
3. **Error Handling**: The `fetch()` itself will only reject on network errors (like a DNS failure or no internet). HTTP errors (like 404 or 500) do not cause rejection. Instead, you must check `response.ok` or `response.status` to handle HTTP-level errors.

GET Requests

A simple GET request:

```
fetch('https://jsonplaceholder.typicode.com/posts
/1')
  .then(response => {
    if (!response.ok) {
      throw new Error(`HTTP error! Status:
${response.status}`);
    }
    return response.json();
  })
```

```
  .then(post => {
    console.log(post);
  })
  .catch(err => console.log('Error:', err));
```

POST Requests

To send data via POST, include a `method` and a body in the
`init` object. Often, you'll also need headers indicating the content
type:

```
fetch('https://jsonplaceholder.typicode.com/posts', {
  method: 'POST',
  headers: {
    'Content-Type': 'application/json'
  },
  body: JSON.stringify({
    title: 'My New Post',
    body: 'This is the content of the post.',
    userId: 1
  })
})
.then(response => response.json())
.then(data => {
  console.log('Created post:', data);
```

```
})
.catch(error => console.error('Error:', error));
```

PUT/PATCH/DELETE Requests

Likewise, other HTTP methods can be used:

PUT (Replace a resource):

```
fetch('https://jsonplaceholder.typicode.com/posts
/1', {
  method: 'PUT',
  headers: {'Content-Type': 'application/json'},
  body: JSON.stringify({ title: 'Updated Title',
body: 'Updated Content' })
})
.then(response => response.json())
.then(updatedPost => console.log(updatedPost));
```

PATCH (Update part of a resource):

```
fetch('https://jsonplaceholder.typicode.com/posts
/1', {
  method: 'PATCH',
  headers: {'Content-Type': 'application/json'},
  body: JSON.stringify({ title: 'Partially
Updated Title' })
})
.then(response => response.json())
```

```
.then(updatedPost => console.log(updatedPost));
```
DELETE:
```
fetch('https://jsonplaceholder.typicode.com/posts
/1', {
  method: 'DELETE'
})
.then(response => {
  if (response.ok) {
    console.log('Resource deleted successfully');
  }
});
```

Handling Different Response Types

- **JSON**:
```
fetch('https://api.example.com/data')
  .then(res => res.json())
  .then(jsonData => console.log(jsonData));
```
- **Text**:
```
fetch('https://example.com/sample.txt')
  .then(res => res.text())
  .then(textData => console.log(textData));
```
- **Blob (binary data, e.g., images)**:
```
fetch('https://example.com/image.png')
  .then(res => res.blob())
```

```
.then(imageBlob => {
    const imageURL =
URL.createObjectURL(imageBlob);
    const img = document.createElement('img');
    img.src = imageURL;
    document.body.appendChild(img);
  });
```

Headers and Request Options

You can pass additional options to `fetch()` to configure requests:

```
fetch('https://api.example.com/secure-data', {
  method: 'GET',
  headers: {
    'Authorization': 'Bearer YOUR_ACCESS_TOKEN',
    'Accept': 'application/json'
  },
  mode: 'cors',
  credentials: 'include',
  cache: 'no-cache'
})
.then(res => res.json())
.then(data => console.log(data));
```

Using Async/Await with Fetch

The Fetch API works seamlessly with async/await for cleaner, synchronous-looking code:

```
async function getData() {
  try {
    const response = await
fetch('https://jsonplaceholder.typicode.com/posts
/1');
    if (!response.ok) {
      throw new Error('Network response was not
OK');
    }
    const data = await response.json();
    console.log(data);
  } catch (error) {
    console.error('Fetch error:', error);
  }
}
getData();
```

Multiple-Choice Questions (with Answers and Explanations)

1. **What does the Fetch API return when a request is made?**

A. A callback

B. A Promise

C. A synchronous response object

D. A WebSocket

Answer: B. The Fetch API returns a Promise that resolves to a Response object.

2. **Which of the following methods is used to parse the response as JSON?**

A. `response.text()`

B. `response.json()`

C. `response.body()`

D. `JSON.parse(response)`

Answer: B. `response.json()` returns a Promise that resolves to the parsed JSON.

3. **What will `fetch()` do if the server returns a 404 error?**

A. Automatically throw an error

B. Return a rejected Promise

C. Resolve the Promise, but `response.ok` will be `false`

D. Reload the page

Answer: C. `fetch()` does not reject on HTTP errors, it resolves the Promise. It's up to you to check `response.ok` or `response.status`.

4. **Which HTTP method is used by default when not specified in the fetch options?**

A. POST

B. GET

C. PUT

D. DELETE

Answer: B. The default method is GET.

5.   **How do you handle network errors with fetch?**

A. By checking `response.ok`

B. By catching the Promise rejection with `.catch()`

C. By checking `response.status`

D. By accessing `response.error()`

Answer: B. Network errors cause the Promise to reject, so you handle them with `.catch()`.

6.   **Which of the following response methods returns a Promise that resolves to a readable stream?**

A. `response.stream()`

B. `response.json()`

C. `response.text()`

D. `response.body`

Answer: D. `response.body` is a ReadableStream, whereas `.json()`, `.text()`, etc. return a Promise for fully read data. `response.body` is not a function, it's a property that exposes a ReadableStream.

7.   **If you want to send JSON data using a POST request with Fetch, which header is most important?**

A. `Content-Length`

B. `Authorization`

C. `Content-Type: application/json`

D. `Accept: text/html`

Answer: C. To send JSON data, set the `Content-Type` header to `application/json`.

8.   **Which of these can `fetch()` accept as its first argument?**

A. Only a URL string

B. A Request object or a URL string

C. Only a Request object

D. A Response object

Answer: B. `fetch()` can accept a URL string or a Request object.

9.   **Which method would you use to clone a Response object?**

A. `response.copy()`

B. `response.clone()`

C. `response.duplicate()`

D. `response.backup()`

Answer: B. `response.clone()` creates a clone of the response.

10.   **What type of data does `response.blob()` provide?**

A. JSON

B. Plain text

C. Binary large objects (e.g., images, PDFs)

D. Form data

Answer: C. `.blob()` provides binary data as a Blob object.

11. **Can `fetch()` be used to make cross-domain requests?**

A. No, it can only be used within the same domain

B. Yes, if CORS headers are properly configured on the server

C. Only if using JSONP

D. Only with a browser plugin

Answer: B. `fetch()` can make cross-domain requests if the server allows it via CORS.

12. **What is the default value of the `credentials` option in `fetch()`?**

A. `credentials: 'same-origin'`

B. `credentials: 'include'`

C. `credentials: 'omit'`

D. `credentials: 'none'`

Answer: C. The default is `omit`, which means no credentials are sent by default.

13. **Which of the following is true about `fetch()` and cookies?**

A. Cookies are always included in fetch requests by default.

B. Cookies are never included.

C. Cookies are included only if `credentials: 'include'` or `credentials: 'same-origin'` is specified.

D. Cookies are included automatically for same-domain requests.

Answer: C. To include cookies, set `credentials` to `'include'` or `'same-origin'`.

14. **If you need to handle very large JSON responses, which approach might be beneficial?**

A. Use `response.text()` and then parse the entire response at once.

B. Use `response.json()` and hope it does not exceed memory.

C. Stream the response and process chunks as they arrive (though `fetch()`'s `json()` does not offer partial reads out-of-the-box).

D. Use `XMLHttpRequest`.

Answer: C. For very large data, streaming the response body and processing incrementally can be better. However, the built-in `json()` method reads the entire body before parsing. A more advanced approach (e.g., using the Streams API) would be needed.

15. **When using async/await with `fetch()`, how do you handle HTTP errors?**

A. With a try/catch block and checking `response.ok`.

B. Just try/catch alone.

C. `await fetch()` will throw on HTTP error automatically.

D. Check `response.json()` first.

Answer: A. Even with async/await, `fetch()` won't throw on HTTP error, so you need to check `response.ok` after `await fetch()`.

16. **What does `response.ok` represent?**

A. It's `true` only if the status is 200.

B. It's `true` if the status code is in the range 200-299.

C. It's true if the body is non-empty.

D. It's true for any successful network request including 404.

Answer: B. `response.ok` is true if the HTTP status is between 200 and 299.

17.   **If you need to send form data with a POST request, how would you do it?**

A. Convert the form data to JSON and send as `application/json`.

B. Use `FormData` object and pass it as the body without setting the `Content-Type` manually.

C. Use `response.formData()` directly in fetch.

D. Attach the form element directly to fetch.

Answer: B. Using a `FormData` object as the request body automatically sets the correct headers.

18.   **Which method is used to cancel a fetch request?**

A. `fetch.cancel()`

B. Using an `AbortController` and calling `controller.abort()`

C. `response.cancel()`

D. There is no way to cancel a fetch request

Answer: B. The `AbortController` API allows you to cancel ongoing fetch requests.

19.   **What does `fetch()` return if the requested resource is not found (404)?**

A. A rejected Promise

B. A resolved Promise with `response.ok = false`

C. Nothing

D. A resolved Promise with a JSON error

Answer: B. It resolves with a `Response` object, but `response.ok` is false.

20.   **How can you handle binary data (like images) obtained via fetch?**

A. With `response.json()`

B. With `response.text()`

C. With `response.blob()`

D. With `response.formData()`

Answer: C. `response.blob()` handles binary data as a Blob.

10 Coding Exercises with Full Solutions and Explanations

1. Simple GET Request

Exercise: Fetch JSON data from `https://jsonplaceholder.typicode.com/posts/1` and log the title.

Solution:

```
async function fetchTitle() {
  try {
    const response = await
fetch('https://jsonplaceholder.typicode.com/posts
/1');
```

```
    if (!response.ok) {
      throw new Error(`Request failed with status
${response.status}`);
    }
    const data = await response.json();
    console.log(data.title);
  } catch (error) {
    console.error('Error:', error);
  }
}
fetchTitle();
```

Explanation: We use `await fetch()` to retrieve the post. After checking `response.ok`, we parse the JSON and log the title.

2. Handling Non-OK Responses

Exercise: Fetch from
`https://jsonplaceholder.typicode.com/posts/9999`
(which does not exist), and if response is not ok, log an error message instead of parsing JSON.

Solution:
```
async function fetchNonExistent() {
  const response = await
fetch('https://jsonplaceholder.typicode.com/posts
/9999');
  if (!response.ok) {
```

```
      console.error('Post not found. Status:',
response.status);
      return;
   }
   const data = await response.json();
   console.log('This will not run for a 404.');
}
fetchNonExistent();
```

Explanation: Since the post doesn't exist, the status will be 404 and response.ok will be false. We handle that before calling response.json().

3. POST Request with JSON

Exercise: Create a new post by sending a POST request to https://jsonplaceholder.typicode.com/posts with a JSON body. Log the returned JSON.

Solution:
```
async function createPost() {
   const response = await
fetch('https://jsonplaceholder.typicode.com/posts
', {
      method: 'POST',
      headers: {'Content-Type':
'application/json'},
```

```
  body: JSON.stringify({ title: 'Hello', body:
'World', userId: 1 })
  });
  const data = await response.json();
  console.log(data);
}
createPost();
```

Explanation: We specify method: 'POST', headers, and body as JSON. The returned data includes the newly created resource.

4. Using Blob to Display an Image

Exercise: Fetch an image from https://via.placeholder.com/150 and display it on the page as an element.

Solution:
```
async function displayImage() {
  const response = await
fetch('https://via.placeholder.com/150');
  const blob = await response.blob();
  const imageURL = URL.createObjectURL(blob);
  const img = document.createElement('img');
  img.src = imageURL;
  document.body.appendChild(img);
}
displayImage();
```

Explanation: After fetching the image as a blob, we convert it to a URL and set it as the `src` of a new `img` element.

5. Using FormData for a POST Request

Exercise: Send a POST request to `https://jsonplaceholder.typicode.com/posts` with form data containing `title=FormTitle` and `userId=10`. Log the response.

Solution:

```
async function sendFormData() {
  const formData = new FormData();
  formData.append('title', 'FormTitle');
  formData.append('userId', '10');
  const response = await
fetch('https://jsonplaceholder.typicode.com/posts
', {
    method: 'POST',
    body: formData
  });
  const data = await response.json();
  console.log(data);
}
sendFormData();
```

Explanation: `FormData` is appended with fields. No need to set `Content-Type` as the browser does it automatically. The server treats it as form submission.

6. Using Headers and Auth

Exercise: Fetch data from `https://jsonplaceholder.typicode.com/posts/1` but pretend we need an authorization header. Log the JSON.

Solution:

```
async function fetchWithAuth() {
  const response = await
fetch('https://jsonplaceholder.typicode.com/posts
/1', {
    headers: {
      'Authorization': 'Bearer some_fake_token'
    }
  });
  const data = await response.json();
  console.log(data);
}
fetchWithAuth();
```

Explanation: We add a headers object to include authorization. Even though this endpoint doesn't require it, the code shows how to do it.

7. Error Handling with Try/Catch

Exercise: Attempt to fetch from an invalid URL `https://invalid-domain.xyz` and catch the error.

Solution:

```
async function invalidFetch() {
  try {
    const response = await
fetch('https://invalid-domain.xyz');
    const data = await response.json();
    console.log(data);
  } catch (error) {
    console.error('Network error:', error);
  }
}
invalidFetch();
```

Explanation: Since the domain does not exist, `fetch` will reject, and the error will be caught in the `catch` block.

8. Checking Response Type

Exercise: Fetch `https://jsonplaceholder.typicode.com/posts/1` and print whether it's JSON or not by checking the `Content-Type` header.

Solution:

```
async function checkContentType() {
```

```
  const response = await
fetch('https://jsonplaceholder.typicode.com/posts
/1');
  const contentType =
response.headers.get('Content-Type');
  if (contentType &&
contentType.includes('application/json')) {
    const data = await response.json();
    console.log('Data is JSON:', data);
  } else {
    console.log('Data is not JSON.');
  }
}
checkContentType();
```

Explanation: We inspect the Content-Type header from the response before deciding how to parse the body.

9. PUT Request

Exercise: Update a post (id=1) via a PUT request to https://jsonplaceholder.typicode.com/posts/1 with new title and body. Log the updated post.

Solution:

```
async function updatePost() {
```

```
  const response = await
fetch('https://jsonplaceholder.typicode.com/posts
/1', {
    method: 'PUT',
    headers: {'Content-Type':
'application/json'},
    body: JSON.stringify({ title: 'Updated
Title', body: 'Updated Body', userId: 1 })
  });
  const updated = await response.json();
  console.log(updated);
}
updatePost();
```

Explanation: We use a PUT request with JSON data to replace the resource at /posts/1.

10. Abort a Fetch Request

Exercise: Create a fetch request to a slow endpoint (simulated with a timeout) and abort it after 1 second.

Solution (Note: This requires a controlled endpoint or a delay simulation. We'll just show the pattern):

```
async function fetchWithAbort() {
  const controller = new AbortController();
  const signal = controller.signal;
```

```
  const fetchPromise =
fetch('https://jsonplaceholder.typicode.com/posts
/1', { signal });
  setTimeout(() => {
    controller.abort(); // abort after 1 second
  }, 1000);
  try {
    const response = await fetchPromise;
    const data = await response.json();
    console.log('Data:', data);
  } catch (error) {
    if (error.name === 'AbortError') {
      console.log('Fetch request was aborted!');
    } else {
      console.log('Error:', error);
    }
  }
}
fetchWithAbort();
```

Explanation: We create an AbortController and pass its signal to the fetch request. After 1 second, we call abort(). The fetch Promise rejects with an AbortError, which we catch and handle.

Conclusion

The Fetch API is a versatile and modern tool for making HTTP requests in JavaScript. It simplifies asynchronous networking and integrates well with newer language features like async/await. Understanding how to handle responses, parse different data formats, and handle errors is crucial for any developer working with web APIs.

Understanding Error Handling in Asynchronous JavaScript

Asynchronous code in JavaScript often involves promises, async/await functions, and other asynchronous constructs. Error handling can differ from synchronous `try...catch`. This guide covers how to handle errors gracefully in promises, async functions, and how `.catch()` and onRejected are used.

Handling Errors in Promises

Promises represent asynchronous operations. They can either:
- **Fulfill** with a value, or
- **Reject** with an error (or a reason).

`.then()` and `.catch()`
- `.then(onFulfilled, onRejected)`: The second argument can handle errors. Alternatively, use `.catch(onRejected)` after `.then()` to handle rejections.
- If a promise rejects, `.catch()` is used to handle that rejection.

Example:

```
fetch("invalid-url")
   .then(response => response.json())
   .then(data => console.log(data))
   .catch(error => {
      console.error("Fetch error:", error);
   });
```

If `fetch()` fails, `.catch()` handles the error.

Handling Errors with async/await

async/await syntax allows you to write asynchronous code that looks synchronous. To handle errors:

- Wrap await calls in a `try...catch` block.
- If the awaited promise rejects, control jumps to the `catch` block.

Example:

```
async function getData() {
   try {
      const response = await fetch("invalid-url");
      const data = await response.json();
      console.log(data);
   } catch (error) {
      console.error("Error caught:", error);
   }
}
```

```
getData();
```
If `fetch` or `response.json()` fails, `catch` block handles the error.

onRejected Callback in Promises

When using `.then()`, you can provide the second argument as an error handler:

```
fetch("invalid-url")
    .then(response => response.json(), error => {
        console.error("Error (then onRejected):",
error);
    });
```

But `.catch()` is more commonly used as it improves readability and chaining.

Promise Rejection Best Practices

- Always handle promise rejections either with `.catch()` or `try...catch` in async functions.
- Unhandled promise rejections can cause warnings and potentially future errors in strict environments.

Examples

Promise with .catch:

```
new Promise((resolve, reject) => {
```

```javascript
    setTimeout(() => reject("Something went
wrong"), 1000);
})
.then(value => console.log(value))
.catch(err => console.error("Caught:", err));
```

Async/Await with try...catch:

```javascript
async function processData() {
  try {
    const result = await someAsyncFunction();
    console.log("Result:", result);
  } catch (e) {
    console.error("Error processing data:", e);
  }
}
```

Re-throwing Errors:

```javascript
async function fetchData() {
  try {
    const res = await fetch("data.json");
    if (!res.ok) throw new Error("Network
response was not ok");
    return res.json();
  } catch (error) {
    console.error("Fetch failed:", error);
    throw error; // re-throw for caller to handle
  }
```

}

Multiple-Choice Questions

1.   **How do you handle errors in a promise chain using `.catch()`?**

A. Attach `.catch()` at the end to handle any rejections in the chain.

B. Use `try...catch` directly on `.then()`

C. `.catch()` only works for synchronous code

D. `.catch()` must be the first method in chain

Answer: A

Explanation: `.catch()` at the end of the chain catches any rejection from the entire preceding chain.

2.   **In `async/await`, how do you handle errors?**

A. Using `.catch()` after `await`

B. Using `try...catch` blocks around `await` calls

C. Errors are always swallowed

D. You cannot handle errors with async/await

Answer: B

Explanation: Wrap `await` calls in `try...catch` to handle errors.

3.   **What happens if a promise rejects and there's no `.catch()` or `then(onRejected)`?**

A. The error is silently ignored.

B. The promise never settles.

C. An unhandled promise rejection warning occurs.

D. The code crashes immediately.

Answer: C

Explanation: Unhandled rejections trigger console warnings, may cause future errors.

4.   **Which is preferred for readability:**
`.then(onFulfilled, onRejected)` **or**
`.catch(onRejected)?`

A. `then` second argument is preferred

B. `.catch()` is typically clearer and more common

C. Both are equally used

D. `onRejected` inside `then` is mandatory

Answer: B

Explanation: `.catch()` is generally more readable and commonly used.

5.   **In async/await, if** `await somePromise;` **throws, where does the error go if not caught?**

A. It's automatically logged

B. It's thrown up to the caller of the async function

C. It's converted to a fulfilled value

D. It's ignored

Answer: B

Explanation: If not caught, it bubbles up to the caller of that async function.

6.   **Can you use** `try...catch` **outside of async functions to handle promise errors?**

A. Yes, if you await a promise outside of async function

B. No, `await` only works in async functions

C. You can try...catch synchronous code only

D. `try...catch` doesn't handle promise errors without `await`

Answer: D

Explanation: `try...catch` is for synchronous code. For promises, `await` is needed in async functions.

7. **What is the effect of `throw new Error("...")` inside async function's `try` block?**

A. It returns the error as a resolved value

B. It rejects the promise returned by the async function

C. It does nothing

D. It logs the error and continues

Answer: B

Explanation: Throwing inside async function `try` block rejects the async function's returned promise.

8. **If multiple `.then()` calls are chained and the first one throws an error, what happens?**

A. Subsequent `.then()` calls still run

B. The chain skips to `.catch()` if present

C. The chain stops entirely without `.catch()`

D. It's converted to a resolved promise

Answer: B

Explanation: Once an error is thrown, it jumps to the nearest `.catch()` in the chain.

9. **If you don't handle a rejection in a promise chain, what could be a consequence?**

A. Silent error

B. Unhandled promise rejection warning or possibly crash in strict environments

C. Automatic retry

D. It turns into success

Answer: B

10.   **onRejected callback in then(onFulfilled, onRejected) is called when?**

A. When the promise fulfills

B. When the promise rejects

C. Always

D. Never

Answer: B

Explanation: The second argument handles rejection.

11.   **Can you use finally() in promises to handle errors?**

A. finally() doesn't receive errors, but runs after resolve/reject

B. finally() acts just like .catch()

C. finally() is only for synchronous code

D. finally() prevents error propagation

Answer: A

Explanation: finally() runs after promise settles, but doesn't handle errors directly, it doesn't get error argument.

12.   **If fetch() fails due to a network error, how do you catch it?**

A. With .catch() on the promise returned by fetch()

B. fetch never fails

C. Use try...catch without async

D. fetch logs automatically

Answer: A

Explanation: fetch returns a promise, handle network errors with `.catch()`.

13.   **In async functions, what is a common pattern for error handling?**

A. `try...catch` around `await` calls

B. Only `.then()` and `.catch()`

C. No error handling needed

D. Using synchronous `throw` without try...catch

Answer: A

14.   **If `await` is used on a promise that rejects, how do you prevent a crash?**

A. Use `await` alone does nothing

B. Wrap `await` in `try...catch`

C. `await` can't handle rejections

D. `await` converts rejection to success

Answer: B

15.   **If you have a `.then()` chain and you want to handle errors at the end, you use:**

A. `.catch()` at the end of chain

B. `try...catch` block

C. Another `.then()` with error parameter

D. `.finally()` only

Answer: A

16.   **If `onRejected` is not provided in `.then(onFulfilled)`, what happens on error?**

A. It throws a runtime error

B. Error is not handled and can result in unhandled rejection

C. It's silently turned into fulfillment

D. It's handled by default error handler

Answer: B

17.   **To re-throw an error after logging inside .catch(),**
what do you do?

A. throw error; inside .catch() callback

B. Just return error

C. .catch() cannot re-throw

D. Call .then() again

Answer: A

18.   **In .then() chains, what if you return a promise that**
rejects in .then() callback?

A. The chain breaks

B. The next .catch() handles the error

C. It's ignored

D. The chain stops completely

Answer: B

19.   **Are synchronous errors in async functions also caught**
by try...catch?

A. No, only asynchronous errors

B. Yes, try...catch inside async handles both sync and async
errors

C. try...catch inside async only catches async errors

D. They must be handled separately

Answer: B

20. **If multiple `.catch()` are chained, which one handles the error?**

A. The first `.catch()` after the error

B. All `.catch()` run sequentially

C. None run

D. The last `.catch()`

Answer: A

10 Coding Exercises with Full Solutions and Explanations

Exercise 1: Basic .catch usage

Task: Create a promise that rejects and handle it with `.catch()`.

Solution:

```
Promise.reject("Error happened")
  .then(value => console.log("Success:", value))
  .catch(err => console.error("Caught:", err));
// Caught: Error happened
```

Explanation: The `.catch()` handles the rejection from `Promise.reject()`.

Exercise 2: Handling fetch errors with .catch

Task: Use fetch on an invalid URL and catch the error.

Solution:

```
fetch('invalid-url')
  .then(response => response.json())
  .catch(error => console.error("Fetch failed:",
error));
```

Explanation: `.catch()` handles network or parsing errors.

Exercise 3: Async/await try...catch

Task: Write an async function that awaits a rejecting promise and catch the error in try...catch.

Solution:

```
async function testAsyncError() {
  try {
    const result = await Promise.reject("Async
error");
    console.log(result);
  } catch (e) {
    console.error("Caught in async/await:", e);
  }
}

testAsyncError();
// "Caught in async/await: Async error"
```

Explanation: The await rejects and `catch` block handles it.

Exercise 4: Re-throwing an error

Task: Catch an error and re-throw it to be handled by another `.catch()` downstream.

Solution:

```
Promise.reject("Initial error")
  .catch(err => {
    console.error("First catch:", err);
    throw err;
  })
  .catch(err => console.error("Second catch:",
err));
```

Explanation: Error is caught first, re-thrown, then caught by second `.catch()`.

Exercise 5: Using finally with errors

Task: Use `.finally()` to run code after promise rejects, and verify error handling still works.

Solution:

```
Promise.reject("Error again")
  .catch(err => {
    console.error("Error handled:", err);
    return "Recovered";
  })
  .finally(() => console.log("Clean up after
settling"));
// Error handled: Error again
```

// Clean up after settling

Explanation: `finally()` runs after promise settles, doesn't affect error handling.

Exercise 6: Multiple awaits in try...catch

Task: Await two promises, second rejects, handle in try...catch.
Solution:

```
async function twoAsyncCalls() {
  try {
    const val1 = await Promise.resolve("Ok");
    console.log("val1:", val1);
    const val2 = await Promise.reject("Fail");
    console.log("val2:", val2); // won't run
  } catch (e) {
    console.error("Error in second await:", e);
  }
}
twoAsyncCalls();
// val1: Ok
// Error in second await: Fail
```

Explanation: The second await throws, caught by catch.

Exercise 7: Using onRejected in then

Task: Provide second argument to `.then()` for error handling.
Solution:

```
Promise.reject("Oops")
  .then(
    value => console.log("value:", value),
    error => console.error("Error handled by
onRejected:", error)
  );
// "Error handled by onRejected: Oops"
```

Explanation: The second argument of `.then()` handles the rejection.

Exercise 8: Conditional error handling

Task: Fetch and if response not ok, throw an error, catch in async/await.

Solution:
```
async function getData() {
  try {
    const res = await
fetch('https://jsonplaceholder.typicode.com/posts
/1');
    if (!res.ok) throw new Error("Response not
ok");
    const data = await res.json();
    console.log(data);
  } catch(e) {
    console.error("Fetch error:", e);
```

```
    }
}
getData();
```

Explanation: Throws custom error if response not ok, caught in try...catch.

Exercise 9: Promise chain with error in the middle

Task: Promise chain: first `.then()` resolves, second `.then()` throws error, final `.catch()` handles it.

Solution:

```
Promise.resolve("Start")
  .then(val => val + " -> then1")
  .then(val => {
    console.log(val);
    throw new Error("Error in second then");
  })
  .then(val => console.log(val)) // won't run
  .catch(err => console.error("Caught in chain:",
err));
```

Explanation: Error thrown in second `.then()` goes to `.catch()`.

Exercise 10: Custom error classes in async function

Task: Throw a custom error in async/await and handle it.
Solution:

```javascript
class CustomError extends Error {
  constructor(message) {
    super(message);
    this.name = 'CustomError';
  }
}
async function doSomething() {
  try {
    throw new CustomError("Custom error
occurred");
  } catch(e) {
    console.error(e.name, e.message); //
"CustomError Custom error occurred"
  }
}
doSomething();
```

Explanation: Async code can throw and catch custom errors as well.

Summary

- Errors in promises are handled with `.catch()` or second argument in `.then()`.
- `async`/`await` allows using `try...catch` for more natural error handling.

- Always handle promise rejections to avoid unhandled rejection warnings.
- `.catch()` in promise chains and `try...catch` in async functions are key techniques.
- Proper error handling ensures robust and maintainable asynchronous code.

By mastering these techniques, you can write resilient JavaScript code that gracefully handles errors in asynchronous operations.

Conclusion

Congratulations on completing **"JavaScript Handbook: Advanced Functions"**! You've taken a significant step in mastering advanced JavaScript techniques that form the backbone of modern web development.

By understanding and applying concepts like higher-order functions, currying, and composition, you've acquired tools that enhance the flexibility, efficiency, and readability of your code. As you continue your coding journey, revisit these principles, experiment with real-world projects, and strive to make your applications robust and scalable.

Thank you for choosing this book as your learning companion. Keep exploring, keep coding, and continue unlocking the full potential of JavaScript!

About the Author

Laurence Lars Svekis is a distinguished web developer, sought-after educator, and best-selling author, renowned for his profound contributions to **JavaScript development** and modern web programming education. With over two decades of experience in web application development, Laurence has become a leading authority in the field, empowering developers worldwide with his clear, insightful, and practical approach to complex coding concepts.

Laurence specializes in **JavaScript, functional programming, asynchronous programming**, and front-end web development. His deep technical expertise, combined with a passion for teaching, allows him to deliver comprehensive courses and resources that simplify even the most challenging programming topics. Through his content, Laurence equips learners with practical skills to build scalable, maintainable, and efficient applications.

With over **one million students worldwide**, Laurence's interactive courses, books, and live presentations have become a cornerstone for developers looking to master JavaScript. His hands-on teaching style, enriched with **real-world examples, coding exercises, and projects**, makes advanced topics like closures, promises, and async programming accessible to learners of all levels.

In addition to being a prolific author, Laurence actively contributes to the broader web development community by sharing insights, fostering collaboration, and mentoring developers. His ability to break down complex technical concepts into simple, actionable steps has earned him a reputation as a trusted and inspiring voice in JavaScript education.

Passionate about solving real-world problems through code, Laurence continues to push the boundaries of modern development. His expertise in JavaScript is especially relevant in today's world of frameworks like **React, Vue.js, and Angular**, where efficient and modular code is essential. Through his books, courses, and presentations, Laurence helps developers unlock their potential and thrive in the ever-evolving world of software development.

To learn more about Laurence's work and access free resources, visit **BaseScripts.com**, where his dedication to teaching and community building continues to shape the next generation of developers.